Like a Misunderstood Salvation and Other Poems

COLLECTION

AVANT-GARDE & MODERNISM

Like a Misunderstood Salvation and Other Poems

AIMÉ CÉSAIRE

Translated from the French and with an introduction by
Annette Smith and Dominic Thomas

Northwestern

University Press

Evanston

Illinois

Northwestern University Press
www.nupress.northwestern.edu

Printed in the United States of America

10 9 8 7 6 5 4 3 2 1

Library of Congress Cataloging-in-Publication Data
Césaire, Aimé.
[Poems. 1994. English]
Like a misunderstood salvation and other poems / Aimé Césaire ; translated from the French and with an introduction by Annette Smith and Dominic Thomas.
p. cm.—(AGM collection)
"Originally published in French as Aimé Césaire: La poésie in 1994, 2006 by Editions du Seuil."
Includes bibliographical references.
ISBN 978-0-8101-2896-5 (pbk. : alk. paper)
I. Smith, Annette (Annette J.) II. Thomas, Dominic Richard David. III. Title. IV. Series: AGM collection.
PQ3949.C44A2 2013
841'.914—dc23

2012041527

♾ The paper used in this publication meets the minimum requirements of the American National Standard for Information Sciences—Permanence of Paper for Printed Library Materials, ANSI Z39.48–1992.

Contents

. . . dying in black and white we fight for what we love, not are.

—Frank O'Hara, "Ode: Salute to the French Negro Poets," 1974

Introduction

These translations of *Solar Throat Slashed* (poems deleted) and *Like a Misunderstood Salvation* promise to generate new and exciting discussions on the groundbreaking work of a giant of twentieth-century literature. This collection has the virtue of presenting an early and a last stage of a poet's course, thus summarizing his entire career and offering readers the rare opportunity to assess Césaire's creative evolution in one volume and to experience the work of someone who was arguably the only French poet writing simultaneously at the crossroads of the avant-garde *and* classicism. Moreover, these poems are politically important; even though they were initially excluded from a French republication of *Soleil cou coupé* in 1961, they are crucial to understanding Césaire's legacy. They remain of tremendous pertinence today as they continue to provide helpful ways of thinking about and contextualizing discussions of individual race and global identities, and of thinking about the links between what Kenyan author Ngũgĩ wa Thiong'o has characterized as "black consciousness" and "social consciousness."[1]

The Collections

Solar Throat Slashed (poems deleted)

The collection *Soleil cou coupé* (*Solar Throat Slashed*) was first published in an in extenso edition in 1948 in Paris by Éditions K. and republished by

Éditions du Seuil in 1961. However, thirty-one poems were deleted from the latter edition and only reintroduced as an annex to the volume under the title of *Cadastre* in the 1994 anthology *Aimé Césaire: La poésie,* edited by Daniel Maximin (Guadeloupean novelist and poet) and Gilles Carpentier.[2] In *Aimé Césaire: The Collected Poetry,* translated by Clayton Eshleman and Annette Smith and published in 1983, a book that is widely accepted as the most important English-language translation of Césaire's work, only excerpts of "Lynch" and "Rain" were included, whereas this new translation includes complete translations of *all* the poems deleted from *Solar Throat Slashed.* Why Césaire deleted those poems and why he decided to include them some thirty-three years later remains, after the death of their author, a matter for conjecture. The general opinion is that Césaire's original decision was motivated by a desire to purge the original collection of local or political references and concentrate instead on more universal content, while moderating their surrealistic style in favor of a more classical one. Whatever Césaire's motivations were, one cannot begin to accurately contextualize the global relevance of his work without including these key components of his œuvre.

Like a Misunderstood Salvation

The second section of this volume includes Césaire's last collection, *Like a Misunderstood Salvation* (*Comme un malentendu de salut*). These poems have a complicated publishing history. "Dyali" was first published by *Présence Africaine* in April 1955; the poems "Obsidian Stele for Alioune Diop," "Passage," "References," "The Virtue of Fireflies," "Course," "Rapacious Space," "Phantasms," "Laughable," and "Configurations," along with "Dyali," and a first version of "The Sleeping Woman Rock" were published in the journal *PO&SIE* in 1989. "Passage," "References," "Supreme Mask," "The Virtue of Fireflies," "Rumination," "Time to Speak," and "Course" were published in a limited edition, illustrated by Moroccan artist Mehdi Qotbi, by Atelier Dutrou in Paris in 1993. Later, in 1994, "Dyali," "Conventicles," "Islands Speak," "Like a Misunderstood Salvation," "Ruminatings of Calderas," "Through," "Favor from the Trade Winds," and all previously published poems were either published or republished in the aforementioned volume edited by Maximin and Carpentier. In addition, a translation of "Dérisoire" ("Laughable") by Clayton Eshleman and Annette Smith appeared in *Sulfur* in the spring of 2000, and translations by Annette Smith of "Parole due" ("Time to Speak"), "Espace-rapace" ("Rapacious Space"),

"Pour un cinquantième anniversaire" ("For a Fiftieth Anniversary"), and "Configurations" ("Configurations") appeared in *Research in African Literatures* in 2006. With the exception of "Dyali," published in the same general period as *Solar Throat Slashed, Lost Body* (*Corps perdu*), and *Ferrements,* between forty-one and forty-six years elapsed after the publication of the first edition (1948) of *Solar Throat Slashed.* It is difficult to know when exactly the poems in *Like a Misunderstood Salvation* were written, especially since a number of them are occasional poems. However, features of style and content make it possible to attribute them to a much later period of Césaire's life.

As is the case in most of Césaire's early poems, we find ample evidence of Césaire's lasting debt to French surrealism. Violence occupies the stage almost constantly, in line with the title of the collection itself, *Solar Throat Slashed,* whether referring to the forced separation from the (however mythologized) motherland of Africa or to the general violence associated with slavery.

Césaire begins his spiritual voyage from a small island covered with luxuriant vegetation that he insists on not only describing but also naming with botanical precision. In *Solar Throat Slashed* we thus encounter passionflowers, ceibas, dragon trees, droseras, ipomeas, balsam (also known locally as "chicken shit"), sumac, and many other tropical plants. In his essay "Poésie et connaissance" ("Poetry and Knowledge"), Césaire had already advocated the benefits for man of becoming a tree and of saying yes like a tree—signifying strength and lasting power rather than passivity.[3] In his "Lettre à Lilyan Kesteloot" (his close friend), he reiterated his need to *name* those plants in order to make his poetry "concrete," anchored in a definite and real ("vivante") geography.[4] However, his island is as violent as it is lush, subject to volcanic eruptions and frequent cyclones demonstrative of a pelean or pelagic force that Césaire extends to the whole universe. His "incandescent" narrator lives in a world populated by monsters in their various exuberant incarnations and dominated by the theme of devouring and deglutition characteristic of folktales and mythologies. This quasi-Rabelaisian but at the same time chthonian omnipresence of the devouring mouth, traditionally meant to frighten (and keep in check) men and children, suggests a similar connotation for Césaire as exemplified by references to Little Red Riding Hood in "Preliminary Question."

Césaire's violence focuses again and again on the various kinds of torture the slaves suffered: knives pushed under nails, legs stretched on the rack, collars, flogging, stabbed eyes spurting, rape, jails, and jailers. He includes two chemicals: antimony (which killed Roman slaves working in the mines) and mercury (toxic by inhalation or ingestion and still nowadays responsible for the deaths of myriad child laborers all over the world). The "buckets of blood . . . donated . . . to the earth" at the end of "Apotheosis" aptly summarize the horrendous debt owed the blacks by the so-called civilized world, a debt extended to a cosmic level in "Forfeit." But, this violence is ambiguous. Under further examination, most of the poems end, whether in a subtle or explicit manner, on a positive note. Césaire leaves the door ajar to the future, fecundating his monsters ("Scalp"), assuming the form of a bull soaring after its slaughter ("Night Crossing"), featuring the gold-helmeted hero that escapes from his scalping ("Scalp"), or else precipitating mankind into a rocky trench but of his liking ("Secret Society"). At times the ending is quite triumphant, as in "Pennon," when the poet refers to Almamy Samory Touré, a legendary combatant of French colonization in Sudan during the nineteenth century. This lifting of the darkness prompted the francophone Haitian writer Dany Laferrière to remark in 2008 in his article "Colère Césaire," that while "Céline went to the end of the night," Césaire goes only to "the end of daybreak,"[5] the phrase punctuating the first pages of the *Cahier d'un retour au pays natal* (*Notebook of a Return to the Native Land*).

The survival (or, more exactly, transcendence) of torture often takes an ironical tinge, as if, laughing up his sleeve, the slave takes pleasure in mocking the master; irony equals freedom. The mummy ("Refinement of a Mummy") observes with satisfaction, it seems, the earth birthing a precious stone in a distant future; in "Transmutation," the narrator surreptitiously grows a series of beautiful hands, some as sumptuous as those of an Aztec emperor; the tray of justice carries three wise men (including a black king) along with spittle in "Compliments of History," and from the sky of "Apotheosis" drops a series of odd objects that end up strewing the poem in a chaos as disrespectful as it is comical.

Evidently sacrifice and rebirth are linked in most mythologies, and one implies the other, an ambivalence characteristic of these poems. The benevolent as well as destructive rain the poet invokes wears Aztec colors that happen to be blue and green, colors of the sky and of spring. The rain appears in the Aztec calendar under the sign of the important deity Tlaloc, a Mesoamerican equivalent of the Hindu Shiva, likewise simultaneously benevolent and destructive. Césaire's lynch is beautiful, and the poet begs the lord executioner to kick, bite, and poison him ("Lynch 1"). He is regaled by the farmers' hatred ("Night Crossing"). Masochism perhaps, but more interestingly the literary espousing of one's indignities so as to cheat the torturer (jailer, executioner, colonial master, the choice is there) from the power to objectify his victim. All readers of Jean Genet will recognize here a device that his characters recur to systematically in order to escape alienation, or as Mario Vargas Llosa wrote of Gustave Flaubert, form is never divorced from life: it is "life's best defender."[6]

Although those poems date from the middle or late 1940s, as a disciple and exponent (however "marooning," by which he means subversive) of surrealistic techniques, Césaire's writing strikingly anticipates the theories of violence and negativity that half a century later the semiotician Julia Kristeva considered essential components of poetic language.[7] This violent negativity, already present in Hegel's ontology and linked by the psychoanalyst Jacques Lacan and his disciples to the rejection of the father's organized, rational, autocratic language (the symbolic, in their terminology), places poetic language within a presymbolic, maternal framework that originates in the body itself and which Kristeva, by association with the Greek dance, names the *chora.* Not only does this language privilege the fluid over the solid and the physical components of speech, such as sounds, alliteration, rhythm, repetition (which would explain why we find many of the poems modeled on litanies), but it also deconstructs the logic of accepted speech, that is in Césaire's case, the speech of the colonizer imposed upon the colonized. Because it tolerates contradictions, ambivalence, obscenity, lies, heterogeneity, rejects solid identity, order, and therefore syntax, poetic speech ends up serving the psychic and political needs of the colonized.

Indeed, Césaire's verses abound in such "physics of language," multiplying chains of alliterations and repetitions, succeeding also in creating phonic simulacra of the object, coining words when necessary, and, in any case, cultivating rare or archaic words that send readers and translators to specialized dictionaries and lexicons. Moreover, his syntax seeks disarticulation, at times under the guise of lingering Latinate constructions remindful of his training and career as a teacher of classical languages. The very proliferation of multiple elements, which never quite fuse in the end, conveys perhaps a desire to welcome foreign entities in the space of the poem while respecting their alterity. In so doing, Césaire establishes a connection with the writings of Walter Benjamin on the duty of the writer to respect the differences between languages decreed by God after the destruction of the Tower of Babel.[8] He also remains faithful to his political and moral commitment to embrace the plurality of the modern world. In his 1956 *Lettre à*

Maurice Thorez (leader of the French Communist Party from 1930 to 1964), he wrote, in response to the universalism of communism, "I do not enclose myself in a narrow particularism. But nor do I want to lose myself in a lifeless [*décharné*] universalism. There are two ways to lose oneself: through walled segregation within the particular and through dilution within the 'universal.' My conception of the universal is of a universal enriched by every particular."[9]

A good example of this generalized tolerance is found in "To the Serpent," one of the longest and most powerful poems in the collection. The serpent, as guardian of sacred places is vengeful ("unforgiving to the cowards") but at the same time friendly. It emanates "frenzy and peace." Associated with ancient chthonian themes (more prevalent in this collection than the solar theme often attributed to Césaire), it represents rebirth on an earthly level ("your successive deaths" presumably referring to the shedding of its skin) but is as well the domain of dead souls, as the serpent Ophion was for the Gnostic Ophites (also known as Serpentinians). We find another of its equivalents in Western culture in the ancient Greek Ouroboros, the serpent devouring its tail, which stood for destruction and regeneration. The serpent's vital power is still honored in many parts of the contemporary world, including Africa.

If we extend the same ambivalence to gender, was not Python a female god and the enemy of Apollo, the god of reason, absolute truth and logic? Many of the poems in this collection bring us back to the theories of poetic language previously mentioned by stressing the androgynous theme said to be its origin. In "Scalp," for instance, the sperm and the (egg)yoke coincide. In "The Rain," the rain is adressed both as a female (laying eggs) and as a male (producing sperm). Furthermore, the substances which Césaire associates often with the torture of the slaves are mercury and antimony. The former is linked in the tradition both with the female principle of a fluid and the male principle of a metal. As for antimony, it was classified by ancient historians as a male and female element, its etymological reference being "against one, against the unity," and thus a principle subverting the centripetal values of patriarchy.

It therefore comes as no surprise that women inspire some of the most eloquent passages in the collection. Césaire does not shy when faced with the realities of the female body (menopause, menses, the obscenity of thighs, the impudence of the vagina), yet in another mode, in "Femme and Flame," "A Few Miles from the Surface," and "Fresh Out of a Metamorphosis," he evokes lyrically and masterfully the intimacy of lovers, inscribing their personal scenes into his accustomed cosmic framework, finding in the union of man and woman one of his best excuses to go from the singular to the universal.[10] Like the entire *Solar Throat Slashed* collection, this group of poems dwells on the necessity to display a prophetic (at times apocalyptic) tone, accompanied by a need or duty to speak up, be it by howling like alouattas ("While in the Heat Naked Monks Come Down from the Himalayas") or as the "final hiccup of a young and rough willfulness" ("Pennon"). The important thing is that in the end the earth's "very clear-speaking thunder" finally be heard ("Apotheosis").

This latter aspect is still prevalent in *Like a Misunderstood Salvation.* In 1993, Césaire officially retired from his seat in the French National Assembly, from where he had actively fought for almost half a century against colonialism and for improvements in the Caribbean and the Third World. But he was still the mayor of Fort-de-France. After stepping down as mayor in 2001 he was considered honorary mayor of the city, continued to occupy his office in the historical township building and remained very popular with his constituents, who affectionately called him Papa Césaire or even at times, with a curiously androgynous pun on the homonyms *maire* and *mère* (the masculine "mayor" and feminine "mother"), "mon maire." When he died, his reputation was that of an easily accessible man and even a helpful resource to the humblest of co-citizens. His mornings remained busy: he continued to receive many visitors, some of them statesmen or important people from other countries, but he also met with people who came with simple practical requests he usually granted, as indeed many of them testified at the time of his death. Nevertheless, in spite of his compassion and modesty, Césaire never abandoned his fairly formal attire and maintained with the public a distance that, one can only surmise, ensured him time to write and think.

This was the proper moment in life to pay homage to old friends. Although eloquent, the poems dedicated to Alioune Diop, Léopold Sédar Senghor, and Édouard Maunick somewhat expectedly celebrate their respective contributions to negritude. In "For a Fiftieth Anniversary," dedicated to Lilyan Kesteloot, Césaire seems to evoke the élan of his lifelong friend in the first part of the poem while, subsequently, as evidenced by the use of a masculine pronoun and of the first person, shifting the focus to a personal and defensive mode directed at his critics. During these years, the poet's afternoons belonged to him alone and, driven by a faithful chauffeur, he used them to revisit his beloved island, stopping to admire the coast or the mornes, revisiting the city of Saint-Pierre, which had been destroyed in

1902 by the quasi-Pompeian eruption of Mount Pelée that razed the town and turned it from the cultural capital of Martinique into a ghost town.[11] More often than not, he simply stopped to admire a tree or a plant, always naming them with exactitude, or just to breathe the air of his island and absorb its special atmosphere. It is this kind of life the poems in *Like a Misunderstood Salvation* reflect. Nevertheless, they tell us of an inner drama. What salvation had been misunderstood and by whom? Or had it perhaps just been botched?

The answer to the first question refers to the attacks, however respectful, Césaire had to withstand from a few of his younger colleagues and former disciples who questioned their elder's political and cultural roles. Had he really saved the French Caribbean people from what could have been a much worse fate? Césaire resented Raphaël Confiant's 1993 book *Aimé Césaire: Une traversée paradoxale du siècle,*[12] in which Confiant positioned himself as the paradigm of the "Créolistes." He reproaches Césaire for having sacrificed the Antilles' political cause (in particular a more independent status within the French Union) in favor of his involvement with Africa and exaggerated Afrocentrism, and for having remained deeply integrated into the French classical culture (as symbolized in Confiant's eyes by Césaire's eternal European three-piece suits). Already in the opening lines of the manifesto "In Praise of Creoleness" ("Éloge de la créolité"), published in 1989 by Jean Bernabé, Patrick Chamoiseau, and Raphaël Confiant, the authors claim to be "neither Europeans, nor Africans, nor Asians, we proclaim ourselves Creoles"[13] and mourn the loss of "créolité" to continental French culture. In response, poems such as "References," "Rumination," and "For a Fiftieth Anniversary" are to some extent subtle self-justifications. Césaire's answer was simple: "A man was here" ("For a Fiftieth Anniversary"), no one else. And does it matter in the long run if *they* (the oblivious wind in "For a Fiftieth Anniversary") now deny that the poet's breath/voice, alone, sufficed in signifying to the whole world and forever that he first cried out "an unforgettable wound"?

If the salvation was botched rather than misunderstood, Césaire's self-reproach might find its way into a poem like "Laughable," in which Césaire pictures himself as a pitiful and obsolete Prometheus, all dimensions of the original model being ridiculously reduced to a trivial level. However, even though he lacked the benefit of hindsight, this was compensated for by a broader vision, the result of political wisdom, or even perhaps of aging. At the end of the poem the old man may very well be lonely, ineffective, confused, and ill understood, but at least he is now able to relish the paradoxical power of his silence. Instead of worrying about the "dogs" that hunt him ("Time to Speak"), he prefers to concentrate, however modestly, on his achievements: avoiding a hemorrhage (a worse political status?) with his "strict saliva" (in other words his poetry); venturing on uncertain roads, nurturing his island, digging and plowing the soil, planting, and waiting for new growth to appear with a peasant's patience ("Course").

Thus, rather than "looking for an alibi" ("References"), Césaire finds much better use for his time, like conversing with the Sleeping Woman Rock, a tender address to one of his favorite sites in which he explores the mysterious, subliminal, yet intense communication one can keep with natural scenes emblematic of some special story or history. If literature had been to him "an essential lung" (quoted by Denis Lefebvre in "Césaire l'incandescent," *L'hebdo des socialistes,* April 26, 2008), it is now nature he espouses with "an ample lungful" ("Time to Speak"). He surveys with delight this minuscule kingdom that he has succeeded in preserving as its "Minister-of-the-pen" ("Rapacious Space"); preserved perhaps for the next generation, as suggested by the appearance of a child for whom he pledges to keep the future undefiled ("Time to Speak"). Such is his mission, an inner "dictate," as he writes in "Rapacious Space." Reassured about his duties, the poet lets his imagination wander amid fantastic trees (in "Rapacious Space") and, in "Ruminatings of Calderas," voodoo-like "great whirlings of shamans and joltings." Soon, it is he that changes form, metamorphosed now into a powerful volcano, a crab impersonating the sun (in "Favor from the Trade Winds"), a pirate, sugarcane (albeit with a panache on his head), or, in "Configurations," a furious whirlwind. Daydreams of an old man or the *jouissance* of a poet who refused to be shackled by the hatred his slave ancestors had felt?[14] In spite of these playful moments, the whole scene remains somber, the eponymous poem ending on a regressing labyrinth, "stingily opened fountains," ultimately a blemish and a blunder ("Like a Misunderstood Salvation").

No wonder, then, that this questionable balance sheet closes on a classical *mise au tombeau,* a genre Césaire had practiced frequently in other collections.[15] This particular *tombeau* is austere enough and befitting the fallen, disillusioned hero of the play *Et les chiens se taisaient* (*And the Dogs Were Silent,* 1956), minus perhaps the noise. The torrents of blood from slavery dwelled upon in earlier works are now a mere blood clot, but also a precious stone. Rather than a monument, the tomb here is a cave, duly modeled on the traditional dwelling of ancient heroes and deities. But this one contains all of life in its smallest fissures, humble and fragile as sand, to be sure, but patiently preserved by the poet and saved from futility by the power of the Word. The reader should focus on this dimension at the end of this collection, the inventory of a disillusioned old man. Disillusioned but not disempowered, for the word is power, a belief repeated in many forms in the collection, "Speaking farther speaking higher raise the sword tree and the sword" ("Islands Speak"), jump-starting the silence. Such was the poet's mission, which the entire third stanza of "Configurations" addresses in a powerful lyrical outburst. The word, the exasperated but benevolent asp (greetings to the serpent again!) of tender human milk, this is Césaire's last word.

The collection *Like a Misunderstood Salvation,* whose lack of punctuation appropriately suggests inscriptions on Roman funerary steles, shows the semiotic and syntactical oddities characteristic of Césaire's poetics: recurring neologisms (*ancreuses,* associated with a ship's anchor *and* with *en creux,* or "hollow"), shifting grammatical categories, intransitive verbs used transitively, the creation of strange pronominal ones, nouns becoming adjectives or verbs, and so forth. Here again, Latin lends a few of its grammatical constructions in the form of absolute ablatives and complex word ordering. The inherent fluidity of the text confronts the translator with frequent dilemmas. For instance, the phrase "le grand retour d'être" in "Configurations" could be read as a Nietzschean "eternal return" in the context of the metamorphosis and reincarnation themes prevalent in the poems. However, the general antithetical structure of this particular text (rising/ebbing, decency/indecency, among others) leads to understanding the "return of being" as antithetical to "the need to be" ("besoin d'être") and to staying in line with the negative connotation of the word for "return" in many French phrases, such as *retour d'âge* (menopause), *sur le retour* (on the wane), *retour de fortune* (misfortune), to mention just a few.

Equally problematic is one of Césaire's frequent practices that one might call kiting. It consists in lifting a word or an image from a familiar idiom and transferring it to a different context. For instance, the "océan d'huile" in the second stanza of "Configurations" is "kidnapped," so to speak, from *mer d'huile* (a totally flat sea), thus justifying the "doldrums" of our translation. Finally, the alliterative series of vowels and soft consonants that are especially effective in this collection have replaced the cyclopean howlings of earlier poems and have been respected as much as possible, as have double meanings (for example, "gravity" and "sign" in "Configurations"), in a desire to do justice to the playfulness that, off and on, relieves the solemnity of texts written by an older but more serene persona.

As Richard Watts has argued:

> the meaning of the text is largely a product of its signifying practices; we read the words on the page, and we derive meaning from what we read. Still, there is no experience of reading that is unmediated. The text is inseparable from the text-object, the book, since the text is inevitably framed by paratextual material of some kind. It is therefore always partially translated before it is read. Although this is true of all texts, the translation that occurs in the paratext to works belonging to a minority discourse is always more intense, since those necessarily contain a higher quotient of "foreignness," and it is this foreignness that translations must deal with.[16]

When it comes to Aimé Césaire, such a description proves all the more apt, and all those who have undertaken to rise to the challenge of translating his work will surely concur. Whole books have been devoted to the task, such as René Hénane's *Glossaire des termes rares dans l'œuvre d'Aimé Césaire* (2004), highlighting the vast range of sources Césaire draws upon, from "biology, to pathology, mineralogy, zoology, botany and more specifically the fauna and flora of the Antilles and the Tropics."[17] For example, many scholars have traced the title *Soleil cou coupé* back to the concluding lines of Apollinaire's poem "Zone," published in the collection *Alcools* in 1913: "Adieu Adieu/Soleil cou coupé" ("Farewell Farewell/Solar throat slashed"). But, as Hénane has shown, the "cou coupé" is also a bird from Senegal "whose gray feathers speckled with white and tinted with red around the neck give it the appearance of a slit throat."[18] Christopher L. Miller has called attention to this dimension of Césaire's poetry: "Wielding the 'miraculous weapon' of literary modernism, the 'malevolent' dark power of language," Césaire "created a new way to look at the slave trade and the world it created."[19]

While corresponding or equivalent terms may remain subject to individual analysis and interpretation, they nevertheless constitute solutions to translation obstacles and roadblocks. In the end, they are steps in the more substantive project of translating Césaire's poetry, because he himself relied so heavily on experimentation and innovation, and his avant-gardist practices helped define new and diverse approaches to literature while also enriching the shelves of francophone literature in hitherto unforeseen ways.[20] Each of the many published translations of Césaire has somehow proved imperfect, constantly calling for revision and clarification as new information emerges or new evidence surfaces, and demonstrated why each concerted effort ends up being such a humbling experience. Recognizing and reckoning with this fact is also, in the long run, the best way to pay homage to Césaire's creative output, of honoring a corpus that cannot be easily reduced to new lexicons.

Aimé Césaire's Legacy and Global Relevance

Most writers eventually come to understand that recognition is a relative concept. Few, however, can ever hope to command the respect and status of Aimé Césaire and emerge as incontrovertible references or subjects of conversation. The French surrealist poet André Breton entitled his preface to the 1943 edition of the *Cahier d'un retour au pays natal* in what arguably remains the most accurate characterization of Césaire: "Un grand poète noir"—"A Great Negro Poet." Certainly this sentiment is echoed in critic David Alliot's appraisal of Césaire: "To this day, *Notebook of a Return to a Native Land* is the most widely read and translated work by a black writer. The same is true for other works by Aimé Césaire that are also available worldwide in several languages,"[21] or in Christopher L. Miller's position that "no other text, before or since, has done so much to review and rethink the French Atlantic."[22]

Born in Martinique on June 26, 1913, Césaire attended the Lycée Louis-le-Grand and the prestigious École Normale Supérieure in Paris. In 1945, he was elected mayor of Fort-de-France and in 1946 deputy to the French National Assembly, where he served until 1993. Given the political nature of his creative works (poems and plays), his outspoken critiques against French colonial practices in works of nonfiction, such as *Discours sur le colonialisme* (1955),[23] his *Lettre à Maurice Thorez* (1956), and his long-standing political career, it might not be surprising that his death on April 17, 2008, also triggered considerable controversy. As Lydie Moudileno has argued, Césaire's death can be best understood in relation to the death of his lifelong friend and intellectual collaborator Léopold Sédar Senghor on December 20, 2001: "top French officials were conspicuously absent at the funeral ceremony in Dakar."[24] Thus, eager to strengthen relationships with its overseas leaders and population, the French state now (over-) compensated for its relative silence seven years earlier by honoring the emblematic figure of Césaire with *obsèques nationales*—a state funeral. "In all French history," Moudileno writes, "only three writers have been honored in such a fashion: Victor Hugo in 1885, Paul Valéry in 1945, and Colette more than half a century ago in 1954. Thus, on April 20, 2008, high-ranking officials of the French political class (including the President and Socialist Party leaders) traveled to Martinique to attend Césaire's funeral. Three days of homage were also organized in the Metropole along with a public celebration in the Latin Quarter of the author's life sponsored by the Secrétariat d'Etat à l'Outre-Mer (the State Secretariat for Overseas Territories)."[25] There is thus something all the more paradoxical about this gesture given that Victor Hugo, the inaugural French writer to be honored in this fashion, just happened also to be Fernand Césaire's—the poet's father's—author of choice for bedtime reading sessions. That some 123 years later he should be the author selected to complete this circle is certainly one whose irony would not have escaped Césaire.

In many ways, Césaire's biography offers a genuine road map through the twentieth century. When he moved to Paris in September 1932, he entered into a stimulating and vibrant world in which a global black consciousness was emerging.[26] The Harlem Renaissance provided an important precursor to thinking about complex questions of race, and the work of Alain Leroy Locke (1885–1954) and the ideas associated with the "the New Negro" were widely disseminated.[27] The National Association for the Advancement of Colored People had been founded as early as 1910, and W. E. B. Du Bois organized the first Pan-African Congress held in Paris in 1919. There was thus a long and established tradition of relocation to the French capital, and subsequent generations of African American artists and writers would find refuge there as racial segregation policies achieved momentum in the United States. Thus, not only were such important cultural icons as Josephine Baker to move to Paris but major writers such as James Baldwin, Chester Himes, and Richard Wright would also establish residency there.[28] "The European metropole was the privileged point of encounter, particularly in the small, ephemeral organizations and periodicals that sprung up throughout the interwar period in Paris and attempted to pursue internationalist alliances with similarly oriented groups."[29] Alongside the African American contingent, subjects from all of France's colonial territories also gathered in Paris, mostly for the purpose of advanced postsecondary education. Aimé Césaire thus had the opportunity to meet several other "diasporic" intellectuals such as Léon-Gontran Damas, Léopold Sédar Senghor, Bernard Dadié, Paul Hazoumé, René Ménil, Jane and Paulette Nardal, and others.[30] The cultural and political dialogue that ensued as a product of these historical conjunctions yielded animated debates on a broad range of issues that included theorization of race, colonial mechanisms, racism, identity formation, Pan-Africanism, independence, and decolonization.[31]

As F. Abiola Irele has shown, "The controlling idea here is the awareness of a particularized experience—historical, social, and cultural—which gives rise to the sentiment of a distinctive identity."[32]

Césaire played a foundational role in these exchanges, creating a number of journals, such as *L'étudiant noir: Journal mensuel de l'association des étudiants martiniquais en France* (a publication for which he was chosen as its editor in chief) in 1934, *Tropiques* (with his wife, the author Suzanne Césaire [née Roussy], René Ménil, Aristide Maugé, and Georges Gratiant) in 1941, and *Présence Africaine* (with Alioune Diop) in 1947. Its editorial board and committee included many of the leading minds of the era, such as Jean-Paul Sartre, André Gide, Albert Camus, Léopold Sédar Senghor, Richard Wright, Paul Hazoumé, Michel Leiris, Bernard Dadié, Abdoulaye Sadji, Georges Balandier, and Mamadou Dia. These efforts culminated in two significant international gatherings, both of which Césaire attended, namely the First Congress of Black Writers and Artists held at the Sorbonne in 1956, and the Congress of Black Writers and Artists held in Rome in 1959.[33] According to Romuald Fonkoua, it was at these gatherings that "Césaire would insist on the role of black writers and artists in the advent of postcolonial societies . . . in defending the liberties of individuals and of the masses, affirm a renewed consciousness of their identity, and thus contribute to their cultural fulfillment."[34]

That "renewed consciousness" was named negritude, a concept inextricably linked today to cultural, literary, philosophical, political, social, and sociological theorizations of race, to the challenge of colonial constructs and stereotypes, and to the affirmation of black identity. Even today, the seismic impact of statements such as "it-is-beautiful-good-and-legitimate-to-be-a-nigger"[35] reverberates; after all, "writing has also served us as the means of a pointed indictment of the European oppressor in the relentless documentation our literature provides for the stark realities of the Black experience as a historical consequence of conquest and domination."[36] Much uncertainty has surrounded the genealogy of the term, and critics have for the most part agreed that "negritude" first appeared in print in the 1939 edition of the *Cahier d'un retour au pays au natal:* "Haiti, where *negritude* rose for the first time and stated that it believed in its humanity."[37] Later in the poem Césaire would elaborate on the term, expanding its references and connections:

> my negritude is not a stone, its deafness hurled against the clamor of the day

my negritude
is not a leukoma of dead liquid over the earth's dead eye
my negritude
is neither tower nor cathedral.[38]

And then Césaire declines a broad range of colonial stereotypes that served to justify the *civilizing mission,* as a pretext to colonial expansionism:

Those who invented neither powder nor compass
those who could harness neither steam nor electricity
those who explored neither the seas nor the sky but who know
in its most minute corners the land of suffering
those who have known voyages only through uprootings
those who have been lulled to sleep by so much kneeling
those whom they domesticated and Christianized
those whom they inoculated with degeneracy[39]

leading the reader by the hand toward the transformational and revolutionary potential of negritude:

And the nigger scum is on its feet
The seated nigger scum
Unexpectedly standing
standing in the hold
standing in the cabins
standing on deck
standing in the wind
standing under the sun
standing in the blood
standing
and
free[40]

However, recent scholarship has been able to convincingly establish the print origins of the term, and in so doing dramatically revise its historical significance. In an article published in 2010, "The (Revised) Birth of Negritude: Communist Revolution and 'the Immanent Negro' in 1935," Christopher L. Miller provided new insights that will take Césaire scholarship in new and exciting directions, a development that underscores the remarkable ways in which his body of work will continue to foster dynamic thinking on so many issues that remain relevant to today's world. "New evidence has come to light; another issue of *L'étudiant noir* has been found; it invalidates the consensus about the origins of *négritude* and raises new questions about the intellectual and political history of the negritude movement."[41] As it has transpired, a facsimile published in a 2008 book by Christian Folocrat (*Negritude Agonistes: Assimilation against Nationalism in the French-Speaking Caribbean and Guyane*) includes Césaire's essay "Conscience raciale et révolution sociale" (first published in *L'étudiant noir,* no. 3, May–June 1935), in which "he uses *négritude* for the first time":[42]

> Thus, before making the Revolution and in order to make the revolution—the true one—a devastating groundswell, not the mere shaking of surfaces, one condition is essential: to break up the mechanical identification of the races, tear up superficial values, apprehend in ourselves the immanent Negro, plant our *negritude* like a beautiful tree until it bears its most authentic fruits.[43]

This discovery proves to be all the more significant because it presents us with an alternative interpretation of *négritude* than had been attached to its 1939 incarnation and therefore gains additional relevance in framing how one would understand Césaire's poetry, including *Solar Throat Slashed* and *Like a Misunderstood Salvation.* As Miller has shown, "The newly rediscovered, earlier negritude . . . is embedded in and indebted to a heavily Marxist, revolutionary discourse" and "teleologically speaking, he was finding his way toward the fuller articulation of negritude"[44] that would take the form of the 1,055-line extended lyric poem, *Cahier d'un retour au pays natal* (*Notebook of a Return to a Native Land*).

Césaire commanded enormous respect from his peers and from successive generations of writers. A cursory glance at a sample of dedications confirms this: Léon-Gontran Damas's "Solde" (1937), Léopold Sédar Senghor's "Lettre à un poète" (1945), and more recently the Nobel laureate Derek Walcott's "Elegy," in which he writes:

> I sent you, in Martinique, *maître,*
> the unfolding letter of a sail, a letter
> beyond the lines of blindingly white breakers,
> of lace-laden surplices and congregational shale.[45]

Francophone Caribbean writers—Patrick Chamoiseau, Maryse Condé, Raphaël Confiant, Suzanne Dracius, Édouard Glissant, Daniel Maximin, Gisèle Pineau, Simone Schwarz-Bart—have been compelled to acknowledge Césaire's immediate influence on their work, even when demarcating themselves theoretically from negritude (and in so doing reaffirming its indisputable importance) in order to develop more Caribbean-centric readings of history through *Antillanité* (Caribbeanness) and *créolité* (creoleness), theoretical models that have called attention to the specificity and diversity of the Caribbean context as a composite identity whose roots are not to be found exclusively in Africa or in slavery.[46]

Françoise Vergès has written several extremely powerful works and essays on French slavery, the slave trade, commemorative practices, and colonialism. If we are to follow the logic of her argument, according to which "the multiple accounts [provided by novelists and poets] assist us in reconstructing the experience of enslavement, a form of exile in which everything had to be erased, and the heritage of slavery itself,"[47] then on center stage one would find Aimé Césaire's work. Partial responsibility for major twentieth-century developments can be attributed to Césaire. Among them one would have to include the 2001 Taubira Law (named after Césaire's counterpart in the French National Assembly, Christiane Taubira, from French Guyana), for which deputies voted to support an official recognition of slavery as a crime against humanity. Article 1 reads as follows: "The French Republic recognizes the Atlantic slave trade and the slave trade in the Indian Ocean as a crime against humanity, as well as slavery perpetrated from the fifteenth century onward in the Americas and the Caribbean, in the Indian Ocean and in Europe, against African, Amerindian, Malagasy, and Indian populations."[48] Later, in 2004, French prime minister Jean-Pierre Raffarin appointed the Comité Pour la Mémoire de L'esclavage (chaired by Guadeloupean novelist Maryse Condé),[49] which provided recommendations, guidelines, and objectives for appropriate commemoration, teaching, and research on slavery and the slave trade.[50] Likewise, fellow Martinican author Édouard Glissant was commissioned by the French government to write a proposal for a *Centre national pour la mémoire des esclavages et leurs abolitions*.[51]

At a time when globalization has compelled us to think seriously about the nature of twenty-first-century relations and to confront disquieting signs of cultural, political, and racial intolerance, Aimé Césaire's work continues to remind us that there are antecedents to the challenges we face and that sustained analysis, persistent questioning, inventiveness, and solidarity remain applicable forms of social engagement. Indeed, as Paul Gilroy has pointed out, "the big issue that we should address in order to evaluate the health of Europe's cultural and political institutions has arisen right at the intersection of the problems to which Césaire directed attention. Race and class have been articulated together, and profound questions concerning the depth and character of European democracy and unity are being posed by nationalist and racist responses to the claims of old settlers, new migrants, refugees, and asylum seekers."[52] Césaire has been—along with fellow Martinicans Frantz Fanon and Édouard Glissant—one of the few francophone theorists whose work has infused the predominantly anglophone field that is postcolonial studies, offering productive comparative frameworks with which to explore the pluridimensionality of colonial and imperial experiences. As racial identities and racial representation continue to be controversial subjects in both the political and social spheres, it is remarkable to observe how Césaire's own positions remain of consequence to current debates.[53]

Césaire's pioneering work and global presence remain undisputed. Several major studies have been published in recent years: Christopher L. Miller's *The French Atlantic Triangle: Literature and Culture of the Slave Trade* (2008), Pierre Bouvier's *Aimé Césaire, Frantz Fanon: Portraits de décolonisés* (2010), and Romuald Fonkoua's *Aimé Césaire* (2010).[54] Each has, in its own manner, provided fresh assessments of negritude in the postcolonial era, new insights on Aimé Césaire's contributions, and helped in the process of defining his legacy. Similarly, with these new translations of *Solar Throat Slashed* (poems deleted) and *Like a Misunderstood Salvation,* we hope to bring new readers into the conversation and in turn to stimulate this conversation in exhilarating and unpredictable ways.

Notes

1. Ngũgĩ wa Thiong'o, *Something Torn and New: An African Renaissance* (New York: Basic *Civitas* Books, 2009), 132.

2. Césaire, *La poésie.*

3. Césaire, "Poésie et connaissance"; Aimé Césaire, "Poetry and Knowledge," in *Lyric and Dramatic Poetry, 1946–82,* trans. Clayton Eshleman and Annette Smith, xlii–lvi (Charlottesville: University Press of Virginia, 1990).

4. Lilyan Kesteloot, *Aimé Césaire* (Paris: Seghers, 1962), 197.

5. Dany Laferrière, "Colère Césaire," http://www.lepoint.fr/actualites-culture/colere-cesaire/249/0/240626.

6. Mario Vargas Llosa, *The Perpetual Orgy: Flaubert and Madame Bovary*, trans. Helen Lane (New York: Farrar, Straus and Giroux, 1986), 240.

7. On Julia Kristeva's theories on poetics, see her "Poésie et négativité," *L'Homme* 8, no. 2:36–63; *La révolution du language poétique: L'avant-garde à la fin du XIXème siècle; Lautréamont et Mallarmé* (Paris: Seuil, 1974), 24, 101–50, 162; and *Polylogue* (Paris: Seuil, 1977).

8. See, for example, Walter Benjamin, *Illuminations* (New York: Schocken, 1969), 75.

9. Cited in Wilder, *The French Imperial Nation-State*, 290.

10. See Annette Smith, "Césaire au féminin: Où et comment chercher la femme dans son œuvre?" in *Aimé Césaire, du singulier à l'universel: Actes du colloque international de Fort-de-France, 28–30 juin 1993*, 377–87 (Tübingen: Narr, 1994).

11. See Césaire, *Nègre je suis, nègre je resterai*, 12.

12. Confiant, *Aimé Césaire*. Miller, in *The French Atlantic Triangle*, 326–39, points to several blind spots and limitations inherent in such a reading of Césaire's work.

13. Jean Bernabé, Patrick Chamoiseau, and Raphaël Confiant, "In Praise of Creoleness," trans. Mohamed B. Taleb Khyar, *Callaloo* 13 (1990): 886.

14. Césaire is cited in André Brink, "Rencontre avec un être humain," *Jeune Afrique* 48 (April 2008): 102.

15. See, for instance, "Obsidian Stele for Alioune Diop," which opens this collection, "The Tomb of Paul Eluard," "Memorial for Louis Delgrès," "In Memory of a Black Union Leader," "Voodoo Ceremonial for Saint-John Perse," and "When Miguel Angel Asturias Disappeared," in *Aimé Césaire: The Collected Poetry*, 325, 331, 339, 375, 377.

16. Watts, *Packaging Post/Coloniality*, 113.

17. Hénane, *Glossaire des termes rares*, 5.

18. Ibid., 46–47.

19. Miller, *The French Atlantic Triangle*, 338.

20. As Jennifer Anne Boittin's research has shown, "They [Césaire and the editorial team at the journal *Tropiques*] eschewed open rebellion, instead using cannibalistic and surrealistic language to transmit messages of dissidence and resistance to Vichy and colonialism." See Jennifer Anne Boittin, *Colonial Metropolis: The Urban Grounds of Anti-Imperialism and Feminism in Interwar Paris* (Lincoln: University of Nebraska Press, 2010), 217.

21. Alliot, *Aimé Césaire*, 245.

22. Miller, *The French Atlantic Triangle*, 325.

23. Césaire's *Discours* was censured immediately upon publication and later withdrawn from the curriculum in lycées, resulting in Césaire himself being banned from making appearances on radio and television.

24. Lydie Moudileno, "Fame, Celebrity, and the Conditions of Visibility of the

Postcolonial Writer," in *Francophone Sub-Saharan African Literature in Global Contexts,* ed. Alain Mabanckou and Dominic R. D. Thomas, *Yale French Studies,* no. 120 (New Haven: Yale University Press, 2011): 65.

25. Ibid.

26. See, for example, Dominic Thomas, *Black France: Colonialism, Immigration, and Transnationalism* (Bloomington: Indiana University Press, 2007).

27. See Edwards, *The Practice of Diaspora.*

28. See Michel Fabre, *From Harlem to Paris: Black American Writers in France, 1840–1980* (Urbana: University of Illinois Press, 1991); Tyler Stovall, *Paris Noir: African Americans in the City of Lights* (New York: Houghton Mifflin, 1996); James Campbell, *Exiled in Paris: Richard Wright, James Baldwin, Samuel Beckett, and Others on the Left Bank* (Berkeley: University of California Press, 2003); Bennetta Jules-Rosette, *Black Paris: The African Writers' Landscape* (Urbana: University of Illinois Press, 1998), and *Josephine Baker in Art and Life: The Icon and the Image* (Urbana: University of Illinois Press, 2007); and Alain Mabanckou, *Lettre à Jimmy* (Paris: Fayard, 2007).

29. Edwards, *The Practice of Diaspora,* 25.

30. Sharpley-Whiting, *Negritude Women.*

31. See Christopher L. Miller, *Nationalists and Nomads: Essays on Francophone African Literature and Culture* (Chicago: University of Chicago Press, 1999), and Wilder, *The French Imperial Nation-State.*

32. F. Abiola Irele, *The African Imagination: Literature in Africa and the Black Diaspora* (Oxford: Oxford University Press, 2001), 20.

33. See V. Y. Mudimbe, ed., *The Surreptitious Speech: Présence Africaine and the Politics of Otherness, 1947–1987* (Chicago: University of Chicago Press, 1992).

34. Fonkoua, *Aimé Césaire.*

35. Eshleman and Smith, *Aimé Césaire,* 83.

36. Irele, *The African Imagination,* 69.

37. Eshleman and Smith, *Aimé Césaire: The Collected Poetry,* 47; emphasis added.

38. Ibid., 67.

39. Ibid., 64–66.

40. Ibid., 80.

41. Miller, "(Revised) Birth of Negritude," 743.

42. Ibid., 744.

43. Ibid., 747.

44. Ibid., 744, 747–48.

45. Derek Walcott, "Elegy," in *White Egrets* (London: Faber and Faber, 2010), 87.

46. See Édouard Glissant, *Caribbean Discourse: Selected Essays,* trans. J. Michael Dash (Charlottesville: University Press of Virginia, 1989), and *Poetics of Relation,* trans. Betsy Wing (Ann Arbor: University of Michigan Press, 1996); and Patrick Chamoiseau, *Écrire en pays dominé* (Paris: Gallimard, 1997).

47. Françoise Vergès, *La mémoire enchaînée: Questions sur l'esclavage* (Paris: Albin Michel, 2006), 196.

48. See "Textes de lois relatifs à la mémoire et à l'histoire," in *La colonisation, la loi et l'histoire,* ed. Claude Liauzu and Gilles Manceron (Paris: Syllepse, 2006), 164–65.

49. See the report drafted by the commission: www.comite-memoire-esclavage.fr.

50. Comité Pour la Mémoire de L'esclavage, *Mémoires de la traite négrière, de l'esclavage et de leurs abolitions* (Paris: La Découverte, 2005).

51. Édouard Glissant, *Mémoires des esclavages: La fondation d'un Centre national pour la mémoire des esclavages et leurs abolitions* (Paris: Gallimard, 2007).

52. Paul Gilroy, *Postcolonial Melancholia* (New York: Columbia University Press, 2005), 140.

53. See, for example, Vergès, "Pour une lecture postcoloniale," and Barack Obama, *The Speech: Race and Barack Obama's "A More Perfect Union,"* ed. T. Denean Sharpley-Whiting (New York: Bloomsbury, 2009).

54. Miller, *The French Atlantic Triangle;* Bouvier, *Aimé Césaire, Frantz Fanon;* and Fonkoua, *Aimé Césaire.* In addition to these scholarly studies, new translations continue to be published. See for example the recent bilingual French-English edition by A. James Arnold and Clayton Eshleman, *Aimé Césaire. Solar Throat Slashed: The Unexpurgated 1948 Edition* (Middletown, CT: Wesleyan University Press, 2011).

Selected Bibliography

Works of Aimé Césaire

Poetry

Cahier d'un retour au pays natal. Volontés, no. 20 (August 1939).
Les armes miraculeuses. Paris: Gallimard, 1946.
Cahier d'un retour au pays natal. Paris: Bordas, 1947.
Soleil cou-coupé. Paris: K., 1948.
Corps perdu. Paris: Fragrance, 1950.
Ferrements. Paris: Seuil, 1960.
Cadastre. Paris: Seuil, 1961.
Moi, laminaire. Paris: Seuil, 1982.
Aimé Césaire: The Collected Poetry. Ed. and trans. Clayton Eshleman and Annette Smith. Berkeley: University of California Press, 1983.
La poésie. Ed. Daniel Maximin and Gilles Carpentier. Paris: Seuil, 1994.

Plays

Et les chiens se taisaient. Paris: Présence Africaine, 1956.
La tragédie du roi Christophe. Paris: Présence Africaine, 1963.
Une saison au Congo. Seuil, 1966.
Une tempête. Paris: Seuil, 1969.

"Conscience raciale et révolution sociale." *L'étudiant noir: Journal mensuel de l'association des étudiants martiniquais en France,* no. 3 (May–June 1935): 1–2.
"Poésie et connaissance." *Tropiques* 12 (January 1945): 158–70.
Discours sur le colonialisme. Paris: Présence Africaine, 1955.
Lettre à Maurice Thorez. Paris: Présence Africaine, 1956.
Toussaint Louverture: La révolution française et le problème colonial. Paris: Présence Africaine, 1961.
Nègre je suis, nègre je resterai: Entretiens avec Françoise Vergès. Paris: Albin Michel, 2005.

Scholarship on Aimé Césaire

Ako, Edward. "*L'étudiant noir* and the Myth of the Genesis of the Negritude Movement." *Research in African Literatures* 15, no. 3 (1984): 341–53.
Alliot, David. *Aimé Césaire: Le nègre universel.* Paris: Infolio, 2008.
Arnold, A. James. *Modernism and Negritude: The Poetry and Poetics of Aimé Césaire.* Cambridge, Mass.: Harvard University Press, 1981.
Bouvier, Pierre. *Aimé Césaire, Frantz Fanon: Portraits de décolonisés.* Paris: Les Belles Lettres, 2010.
Cailler, Bernadette. "Aimé Césaire: A Warrior in Search of Beauty." *Research in African Literatures* 41, no. 1 (Spring 2010): 14–32.
Confiant, Raphaël. *Aimé Césaire: Une traversée paradoxale du siècle.* Paris: Stock, 1993.
Dash, J. Michael. "Aimé Césaire: The Bearable Lightness of Becoming." *PMLA* 125, no. 3 (May 2010): 737–42.
Delas, Daniel. *Aimé Césaire.* Paris: Hachette, 1991.
Edwards, Brent Hayes. "Aimé Césaire and the Syntax of Influence." *Research in African Literatures* 36, no. 2 (2005): 1–18.
———. *The Practice of Diaspora: Literature, Translation, and the Rise of Black Internationalism.* Cambridge, Mass.: Harvard University Press, 2003.
Eshleman, Clayton, and Annette Smith, eds. and trans. *Aimé Césaire: The Collected Poetry.* Berkeley: University of California Press, 1983.
Folocrat, Christian. *Negritude Agonistes, Assimilation against Nationalism in the French-Speaking Caribbean and Guyane.* Cherry Hill, N.J.: Africana Homestead Legacy, 2008.
Fonkoua, Romuald. *Aimé Césaire.* Paris: Perrin, 2010.
Garraway, Doris L. "'What Is Mine': Césairean Negritude between the Particular and the Universal." *Research in African Literatures* 41, no. 1 (Spring 2010): 71–86.
Hale, Thomas A. *Les écrits d'Aimé Césaire: Bibliographie commentée.* Montreal: Les Presses de l'Université de Montréal, 1978.

Hénane, René. *Aimé Césaire, le chant blessé: Biologie et poétique.* Paris: Jean-Michel Place, 1999.

———. *Césaire et Lautréamont: Bestiaire et métamorphose.* Paris: L'Harmattan, 2006.

———. *Glossaire des termes rares dans l'œuvre d'Aimé Césaire.* Paris: Jean-Michel Place, 2004.

Hopquin, Benoît. *Ces noirs qui ont fait la France: Du chevalier de Saint-George à Aimé Césaire.* Paris: Calmann-Lévy, 2009.

Irele, F. Abiola. *The African Imagination: Literature in Africa and the Black Diaspora.* Oxford: Oxford University Press, 2001.

———. "Homage to Aimé Césaire." *Journal of the African Literature Association* 1, no. 1 (2007): 246–49.

———. *The Negritude Moment: Explorations in Francophone African and Caribbean Literature and Thought.* Trenton, N.J.: Africa World Press, 2011.

Kesteloot, Lilyan. *Black Writers in French: A Literary History of Negritude.* Trans. Ellen Conroy Kennedy. Philadelphia: Temple University Press, 1974.

Kesteloot, Lilyan, and Barthélemy Kotchy. *Aimé Césaire: L'homme et l'œuvre.* Paris: Présence Africaine, 1993.

Larrier, Renée. "A Tradition of Literacy: Césaire In and Out of the Classroom." *Research in African Literatures* 41, no. 1 (Spring 2010): 33–45.

Leiner, Jacqueline. *Aimé Césaire: Le terreau primordial.* Tübingen: Narr, 1993.

Mbom, Clément. *Le théâtre d'Aimé Césaire; ou, La primauté de l'universalité humaine.* Paris: Nathan, 1979.

Miller, Christopher L. *The French Atlantic Triangle: Literature and Culture of the Slave Trade.* Durham: Duke University Press, 2008.

———. "The (Revised) Birth of Negritude: Communist Revolution and 'the Immanent Negro' in 1935." *PMLA* 125, no. 3 (May 2010): 743–49.

Monga, Célestin. *Nihilisme et négritude.* Paris: Presses Universitaires de France, 2009.

Moutoussamy, Ernest. *Aimé Césaire: Député à l'Assemblée nationale, 1945–1993.* Paris: L'Harmattan, 1993.

Murdoch, H. Adlai, ed. "Aimé Césaire, 1913–2008: Poet, Politician, Cultural Statesman." Special issue, *Research in African Literatures* 41, no. 1 (Spring 2010).

Nesbitt, Nick. "History and Nation-Building in Aimé Césaire's *La tragédie du Roi Christophe.*" *Journal of Haitian Studies,* no. 3/4 (1997/98): 132–48.

———. "The Incandescent I, Destroyer of Worlds." *Research in African Literatures* 41, no. 1 (Spring 2010): 121–41.

Ngal, Georges. *Aimé Césaire: Un homme à la recherche d'une patrie.* Paris: Présence Africaine, 1994.

Réjouis, Rose-Myriam. *Veillées pour les mots: Aimé Césaire, Patrick Chamoiseau et Maryse Condé.* Paris: Karthala, 2005.

Rosello, Mireille. "The 'Cesaire Effect,' or How to Cultivate One's Nation." *Research in African Literatures* 32, no. 4 (Winter 2001): 77–91.

———. "'A Thousand Bamboo Fangs down My Throat': Césaire's *Cahier d'un retour au pays natal.*" *PMLA* 125, no. 3 (May 2010), 750–55.

Scharfman, Ronnie Leah. "Aimé Césaire: Poetry Is/and Knowledge." *Research in African Literatures* 41, no. 1 (Spring 2010): 109–20.

———. *Engagement and the Language of the Subject in the Poetry of Aimé Césaire.* Gainesville: University of Florida Press, 1987.

———. "Homage to Aimé Césaire, 1913–2008." *Callaloo* 31, no. 4 (2008): 976–80.

Senghor, Léopold Sédar. *Anthologie de la nouvelle poésie nègre et malgache.* Paris: Presses Universitaires de France, 1948.

Sharpley-Whiting, T. Denean. *Negritude Women.* Minneapolis: University of Minnesota Press, 2002.

Smith, Annette. "A Man Was Here: Aimé Césaire Revisited." *Research in African Literatures* 37, no. 2 (2006): 125–40.

Songolo, Aliko. *Aimé Césaire: Une poétique de la découverte.* Paris: L'Harmattan, 1985.

Thébia-Melsan, Annick, ed. *Aimé Césaire, le legs.* Paris: Argol, 2009.

Toumson, Roger, and Simonne Henry-Valmore. *Aimé Césaire: Le nègre inconsolé.* Paris: Syros; Fort-de-France: Vents des Îles, 1993.

Towa, Marcien. *Poésie de la négritude: Approche structuraliste.* Sherbrooke, Quebec: Naaman, 1983.

Vergès, Françoise. "Pour une lecture postcoloniale de Césaire." In *Nègre je suis, nègre je resterai: Entretiens avec Françoise Vergès,* by Aimé Césaire, 71–136. Paris: Albin Michel, 2005.

Walker, Keith. "The Transformational and Enduring Vision of Aimé Césaire." *PMLA* 125, no. 3 (May 2010): 756–63.

Watts, Richard. "Aimé Césaire's *Cahier d'un retour au pays natal* and Its Displacements." In *Packaging Post/Coloniality: The Manufacture of Literary Identity in the Francophone World,* 99–115. Lanham, Md.: Lexington Books, 2005.

Wilder, Gary. *The French Imperial Nation-State: Negritude and Colonial Humanism Between the Two World Wars.* Chicago: University of Chicago Press, 2005.

———. "Untimely Vision: Aimé Césaire, Decolonization, Utopia." *Public Culture* 21, no. 1 (2009): 101–40.

Wilks, Jennifer. "Writing Home: Comparative Black Modernism and Form in Jean Toomer and Aimé Césaire." *Modern Fiction Studies* 51, no. 4 (Winter 2005): 801–23.

Like a Misunderstood Salvation and Other Poems

Solar Throat Slashed
(poems deleted)

Lynch 1

Why does the spring grab me by the throat? what does it want from me? even if it were short of spears and flags! I boo you spring for displaying your one blind eye and your foul breath. Your stupration your vile embraces. With patches of jungle (fanfare of advancing saps) your peacock tail fans out turning tables but my liver is more acid and my venefice stronger than your maleficence. Lynch is six o'clock in the evening in the oozing bayous it is a black kerchief waved atop the mast of a pirate ship it is the point at which the nail is strangulated by a carmine insertion it is the pampa it is the queen's ballet it is scientific sagacity it is the unforgettable coit. O lynch salt mercury and antimony! Lynch is the blue smile of a dragon at war with angels lynch is an orchid too beautiful to bear fruit lynch is a mere preamble lynch is the wind's hand slaughtering a forest whose trees are gallnuts brandishing the raw flame of their castrated phalluses, lynch is a hand dusted with the powder of precious stones, lynch is a release of hummingbirds, lynch is a lapsus, lynch is a trumpet call a gramophone's cracked record a cyclone's tail whose train is carried by pink-beaked rapacious birds. Lynch is a lush chevelure which fear brushes back over my face lynch is a temple destroyed by roots and girthed by the virgin forest. O lynch lovable companion beautiful spurted eye wide opened mouth mute save when a branle fills it with delirious snot, on your loom, lightning, weave to perfection a continent bursting into islands an oracle sliding into centipedal contortion a moon that posts in the breach the sulfur butterfly rising in the scanty loophole of my murdered hearing.

Devourer

The mollusks' shield
the ants' mandibles
the full display of mimesis eclipsing the masks of
phasms and pharaohs
the dialectic of copper
Aldebaran the early riser
could it be that an ill-cast leaf
scattered by the wind
calls head or tails with life and death
go turtle turned onto its back by the sand's perfidious hand
iconoclastic clast thunder of the nameless no
buck and belfry
date chosen for all great spring offensives
runner
forerunner
I've eaten my prey
and my eyes have grown like yams from an unworked field
my eyes are harder than stone
my eyes have crucified stoned flogged my brain
my brain
comes and goes
in a white smock of logarithms
and since we are on the subject of mental economy
hear this devourer
space and time amicable serpents pincher against pincher fornicate too
well to exhaust their venom vesicle spawning magnificent umbels and
mushrooms in a face voluble with silence and echo
the distribution of the heat intensifies in collective ratio along the rod I
heat up and fecundate with the frantic sap of my breathing

Rain

After I had visited the most famous sites of history by iron by fire by
cinder after I had by cinder by fire by the earth and the stars wooed to
the exacting protoplasms field with my wild dog and leech claws
just as was customary in the old days I found myself in the midst of a
factory of viper knots in a ganges of cacti in an elaboration of pilgrimage
prickles—and as in the old days I was slabbered by cocks and tongues
born a thousand years before the earth—and as in the old days I said
my morning prayer the one that protects me from the evil eye and that I
address to the rain under the Aztec color of its name

Rain that so gently cleanses the earth's dusty vagina with a perverse
injection
All-powerful rain that slits fingers of rock from the chopping block
Rain that sates an army of worms better than would a forest of mulberry
trees
Rain genial strategist that pushes onto the air's window your army of
innumerable zigzagging ramparts guaranteed to surprise the best-guarded
boredom
Rain wasp nest fine milk for the piglets we are
Rain I see your meshes are a continuous explosion of fireworks of
crackling hurrahs
your hair of false news immediately denied
Rain that in your most reprehensible outbursts would not forget that
the Chiriquí maidens suddenly pull out of their night-woven bodices a
lantern made of tantalizing fireflies
Inflexible rain that lays eggs whose larvae are so proud nothing can force
them to pass aft of the sun and salute it in the fashion of an admiral
Rain that is a display of fresh fish behind which the courtly races hide out
watching the filthy-footed victory go by
I salute you rain queen in the depth of the eternal many-handed goddess
whose destiny is unique you sperm you brain you fluid
Rain capable of anything except washing away the blood running on the
fingers of
those peoples' assassins caught under the high timbers of innocence

Secret Society

From the lagoon a smell of blood rises along with an army of flies
spreading among women the news of fraudulent menopausal treasures
the crime's headquarters settled quite comfortably on the route of history
whose epilepsy has never been so pronounced than nowadays when each
inscription becomes an adventure each one of its letters blowing up like a
pack of cartridges
a kindred dust leads to weeks that are the sliding grooves of a guillotine
in front of which the public prosecutor mounts guard
in any case the body's rise and fall indicate all along the phase reached by
the always difficult digestion of geological avatars
we have no use for moles who swelled up the earth in a seasonal outbreak
of rebellion
we have no use for the sun it is a raped girl afraid to go home in its place
a counter rain of sand and mud whose offensive over the cities imitates
the perfect chaos of polarized light bands
such as it may be
in spite of the almond-colored antelopes gathering after a long run in the
dawn of palm trees formed by tears along beloved necks and never to be
dispersed by the sagacious hand of words of solace

(no more than a superstition would ever cleave the fine tree of idolatrous
hearts promised to the axe regardless of the blood staining the executioner's
blocks and throwing the premature flower bouquet of a scalp across its mask)

north wind
and cutlasses of stars
with the convex satellites let us exchange
the little beneficial salute
we exchange with the snow bunting sunlit only for us down from the
delicate dormer windows out of which under a laconic sky the antidote
usually launches
the train of lifeguards
rushed as I please to the bottom of the rocky mule track of an unmarked
catastrophe

In view of Césaire's predilection for words of classical origin and in the absence of any zoological references to "amygdale antelopes," we are translating amygdale as "almond-colored," staying in line with the Greek amygdale, whose meaning is "almond."

Night Crossing

Daring is what will least likely comfort us
here is the animal alloy of muscle and voice in the day's rainy report
under the *plus* sign flown over by a squadron of petrels
Thanks to the farmers who regale me with hatred painted on their faces
the days settle only on the shoulders of women well beyond sleep
Storm or rain
the beaks that delivered me to the mercy of the scream
will take them to a proper ending

Covered with fresh brain
I already rise much faster
silence
like the bull under the hammer
it is a kiss gathering lips
from the print of our hooves

Transmutation

A tree pushes its wrangle of contorted pipe against a wall in the absence
of any objective reference cataracts have hung from the windows the
linen sanitary women stain during their menses so that nothing becomes
more personal than the pillage of time
only the prostitutes' tawed necks still give an idea of eternity
I explain in vain I am not at fault they leave me to myself
forbidden is what a storm forever announced forever postponed yells out
at me incessantly
feeding all the nightmarish ups and downs to our crowds' unconscious
Fortunately no one noticed I had noticed that I have hands to keep
me company I have my ape's tail hands I have booby trap hands I have
murderer's hands I have sleepwalker's hands and at times when the lapsed
remorse arisen from Atlantis throbs in my pulse I have seashell hands
I also have guano hands so beautiful people call them Sierra Nevadas I
have my pigeon-vole hands I have bell diver's hands I also have hands to
rock to sleep the small children who come to me for my smartest trick
consists in trying to stop myself I have the hands of a righteous man
prevented by mildew from ever reaching maturity my incendiary hands
my bicolor hands my prickly heat hands my hand generally speaking
ordinary my pearl divers' hands that are used to the depth
For rainy days I have my strange sea lions' hands I will not describe as
that would be sacrilegious
On holidays I have those sumptuous hands the ancient emperor wore in
Cuzco to welcome the sun I have mirror hands meant to set my hands on
fire to serve as scarecrow for the solstice birds

Dwelling 1

Fuck you jailer
fever the poniard of razzias in its teeth
fever the language of torrents in its teeth
fever thoroughbred gentle hawk
precedes me in its palanquin
Dwelling made of defeats
dwelling made of live steerage
dwelling made of passionflower
dwelling a hundred times made and unmade
dwelling made of shark teeth
ha hallowed dwelling made of god's thunder and lightning
of the secret saps asleep in great ceibas
the scream that curses no longer hangs over me
the shackle pain hindering our shanks
the collar pain heavy on our shoulders
all that has dissipated stripped like this ear of grain
dissipated the way the cove fastens the fair weather light
to the boisterous bowl of the sea
stripped like you Volcano which from atop your crime rushes into suicide
to join your accomplices to be born pensive and patient porpoises
in the depth of the sea

Ceiba is the silk-cotton tree of the West Indies.

The Sun's Stab in the Back of Unsuspecting Cities

And I saw a first beast
it had a crocodile's body horsy legs a dog's head but upon a closer look
rather than buboes those were scars left by storms at different times on a
body long tested by obscure ordeals
its head as I said was that of those mangy dogs one sees roaming around
volcanoes in cities that men haven't dared rebuild eternally haunted by
the souls of the departed
and I saw a second beast
it was lying under the branches of a dragon tree on both sides of his
fawn's muzzle two rostra inflamed in their pulp stretched out like
mustaches
I saw a third beast which was a worm except that a strange will propelled
it into a narrow length and it stretched out on the ground constantly
losing and growing again annuli one would never have imagined it strong
enough to carry and which swiftly passed life to one another like a most
obscene password

Then my words spread out in a clearing of rudimentary eyelids, velvet on
which the fastest shooting stars suckle their jennies

the splattered colors shifted delivered by the veins of a nocturnal ogress
O the house built on rock the woman frigid in bed the catastrophe
lost like a needle in a haystack a rain of onyx and broken seals fell on a
monticule that no priest from any religion had ever named and whose
effect can only be compared to a star's flogging of a planet's rump
to the left forsaking the stars arranging the design of their numbers the
clouds anchoring their reefs in a nonexistent sea the black heart snuggled
in the heart of the storm
we swooped down over tomorrow our pockets full of the sun's most
violent stab in the back of unsuspecting cities

While in the Heat Naked Monks Come Down from the Himalayas

Formidable match the mosquitoes' grapeshot spiraling up from the
coastal fens good manners feigned by the swarthy-pawed brutishness of
the wild boars' lairs

Formidable match the great rivers which for the vermin split their thighs
open
most obscene blue lips spurting a vagina's lewd cackle

Formidable match the pollens' mushy faces crashing in the conspiring
wind and under the tunnel formed by big cats' shoulders the chimney
spewing jewels of eyes more tender than the grain that grows around
them

Formidable monster against monster
yours whose body is a statue made of redwood sap
whose spittle is a chick's piss
mine whose sweat is a bile jet from a caiman

like a night raining the howls of alouattas may I eject them at last from
my so tender agaric's chest

Indecent Behavior

Harsh night starless thrash night. I don't get along with space. Doesn't matter. Night filthy rag mad tree I don't get along with Time. Does it matter? Farther than the mirror farther than the life relived in an accident when it rushes back at great speed farther than forgotten cities farther than rituals with lost meaning farther even than the ostrich carrying away the letters I pretend not to write farther than my little horse I jealously hide for it has left all breeds behind farther than the gold coins a cerebral sun spills thinking of slums farther than the long white gloves donned by the summits to welcome the wind
your eyes, Monster, plunge them into a well-founded abyss fed from a monsters' breeding pond
I don't get along with space don't get along with Time. Doesn't matter.
Through the voyage haunted by high fumigations of flogging on a pavement made of little wrecks
pushing through villages where allerions vegetate enshrined like saints in the beautiful postures of malaria
tottering—at his belt a clinking of keys which among doors open only that of the pythons corridor the same one mind you leading to the bad weather invariably coming from the Atlantic—a beggar rings the bell on the street which from indifference it seems encircles the night's massive energy with rock salt
while the compact masses of pirate icebergs tend towards Ostend

Laissez-Passer

Easy extension of deglutition by the gigantic obscene mouth of a brown-belly marsh
in a contented gunk gooey droseras listening in their lips to what fraternal news
their days are indispensable on this world entangled in too many smokes
from breaths that mask the storm's peppery spirit

Lean lean over the abyss over the vertigo
lean lean over the void
lean lean over the fire

But even high in the sky I find a thousand sharpened knives a thousand lasso hooks a thousand clerical crows

howl strike the rock as for the earth I people it with fish
let flags be hoisted on factories
ring your cohort ring your renewed blaze
ring your silver canopy
ring the array and the disarray
ring your lightning rod breakers
ring your onyx hooves
ring your spidery horizon
ring your cassolettes
ring your small glasses twisted by the disaster
ring your moans
ring your grenade splinters
Along the meridians I support the muffled progress of the opulent pilgrims rabid forests have turned into
commotion
Greenland
disdainful hyenas that sniff at me I am not in the desert! the air stops I hear the squeaking of the poles around their axle the air rustles I watch helplessly my mind going feral the air brings me the Zambezi
The many-boned bamboos resemble the skeleton of a huge fish from geological eras planted as a totem by an extinct tribe.

Solid

Goddamn it they have secured the universe and everything weighs—everything—the gravity's plumb line having settled on the facile foundation of solidity—the uranium veins the gardens' statues perverse amours the street that only feigns being fluid not to mention the river with its pace more sluggish than my feet no exception for the sun which stopped its clouds now forever fixed. "Ten-shun!" it is by the way the order that resounds constantly from one end to the other of this strange army of despair. The world becomes fixed. The stone is fixed. The universal false move is fixed and tell me about your crazy girl manners encircled by the world that encircles a river in which each human couple is ordered to dip twice and whence moreover the bona fide bovine of debacle with its ranch of crosiers and roots will never emerge.
I am a stone covered with ruins. I am an island hooded with guano. I am a pyramid erected by an immemorially disappeared dynasty an elephant herd a mosquito sting a small town aggrandized by crime unless it be by the Pacific War or the Atlantic Charter. There are people claiming that they could rebuild a man from his mere smile. That is why I make sure not to leave my teeth impressions on the putty of the air.
Face of man you will not budge
you are caught in the ferocious graphs of my wrinkles.

Femme and Flame

A lump of light descending the source of a glance
the twin shadow of the brow and the rainbow on the face
and all around
who goes there angelical
and ambling
Woman what's the weather like
what's the weather like who cares
my life is always one step ahead of a hurricane
you are the morning melting on the beacon a pebble of night
between its teeth
you are also the flight of seabirds
you who are the wind through the briny ipomeas of knowledge
stealing in from another world
Woman
you are a dragon whose beautiful color scatters and darkens
until becoming the essential substance of things
I am used to brushfires
I am used to brush rats to ashes glossy ibises
to the flame
Woman pliable as foresail beautiful revenant
helmet of seaweed of eucalyptus
the dawn you know
easy along the hull
most savvy swimmer

Compliments of History

Ogooué maidens do me the favor
of a so-called new star
of a priest atop the sea aiming a kind of blunderbuss
of a twenty pesetas and ten ave marias torture chamber
so that I pry off all your bad thoughts
so that I excise your bad wounds my little friend
seisms it is my turn
volcanoes give me fire
fire beasts hurl me your claws
to defrock the demons breathing in your breath
my great friend to blow up the perverse waters flowing on my cheek into, yes, smithereens of bombs my cheek the one touching yours astride the world's foul roof where from their progress a fireman's truck springs up at once transformed by blood into the gold helmets are made of

and defying the steps in Hyde Park and in the Bank annex Place de la République here are two hollow cavities: two eyes meant to congeal the clouds which most attentively
watch as they would the sight of a touching urchin the lewd beginning of the loutish year
and the blood which in any case ebbs very fast
from an excise officer's kick from a lead cover
from a string of piastres from a husked rice paddy
bringing cheeses of spittle the carat of insult
and Three Wise Men
onto the scale of justice

A Few Miles from the Surface

The tip of the cone of shade on our Brazil cheeks
during the solar eclipses
so blissfully joyous as in the long mating
of a tree and a sailboat
in the vestibule of a category-one cyclone
Woman
give me your eagle eyes
your glorious bird eyes
your eyes of an incendiary bird leader of souls
and how I relish in the blood of disaster running
in the veins of a ten-story house at the sublime minute
before its collapse at exactly three o'clock in the afternoon

Scalp

It is midnight
the witch doctors have not yet arrived
the mountains have not melted
how many times must I tell the earth
not to settle down lest it would get sunstruck?
Shall I strangle myself with my murmurs plaited into an ivy rope?
fishes you gatherers of water and its receptacle
it is above your heads that I speak
like the stars and the earth in the honeyed spittle of its bad dreams
it has given birth beneath us

'Tis true amidst the racket of fat cockchafers I planted my nails into a
cyclone's flesh
until spurting a sperm's new yolk
flinging myself to its underbelly to measure
my rut

Now
by rape's congealed blood
between two thieves
I know when
which one is dying
which one is walking
But *one* but *I*
snuggled in the tuft that benumbs me
and by the mercy of dogs
under the innocent wind loosening lianas
hunting hero helmeted with a golden bird

Apotheosis

Tracking my steps
in the heat of the ill-inscribed temple of a scar
this distance always increasing
my good-for-nothing lantern
all I was able to gnaw from walls (diaphragm formed by the sea slug
throughout the day)

hold on there'll fall on me gold nuggets and swallow nests
there'll fall a wave of crotales and cinders
there'll fall this etui where I hide my wisdom tooth

this bundle of leaves which in my compact sweat's ferocious camouflage
prevents me from hearing
when walnuts are thrashed in the forever blue fields
of lands carried here by the flood
in a scattering of cesspools
amidst the moraine's choirboys
under pearly daggers meant to brand the foreheads and heavens' trumpets
sounding to the red of their eyes

From there will fall a tsetse cake for the Te Deum
a carcass lying in the sand
an imperial eagle handcuffs a glass bead necklace
there'll fall enough of them to raise the level of the Thames
and a cockatoo for the pope
There'll always fall something a police snitch a sexton a telephone pole a
clove
And let's throw in the prayer of a chalcedony dust the dead leaf the shore
shrubby from an ill-diluted blood the faunae recreated from the track by
the tiger's meager and tentative light
There'll fall a red herring

Why (to hell with that scruple) not squeeze the placid time in again and
again until all the buckets of blood we donated drop onto the earth
drunk
at last along with its very clear-speaking thunder

dwelling made of heavens know what
dwelling made of saber splinters
dwelling made of chopped heads
dwelling made of grains of the flood's rain
dwelling made of male harmonicas
dwelling made of green water and female ocarinas
dwelling made of a fallen angel's feathers
dwelling made of tufts of giggles
dwelling made of alarm bells
dwelling made of hides and eyelids
dwelling made of mustard seeds
dwelling made of the fingers of fans
dwelling made of a ceremonial mace
dwelling made of a deluge of dainty eyelashes
dwelling made of an epidemic of drums

what face would we have if we did not defy the sea with a kick
more resounding than our froglike hearts

Dwelling made of chicken shit
dwelling made of poisonous sumac
dwelling made of feathers for a hummingbird's crest

Jailer don't you see my eye always in my clenched fists screaming that my stomach rises to my mouth and feeds it a flight of roaches spawned from its mulsh of mucus?

Beautiful angel inner erosion mine yours pardon is a pariah to be banished from our sight but my anger alone brings me the pungency of your odor and its handful of keys.

Empowered by it rise as I rise from it to the daylight.

Jailer with my clenched fists, here I am, with my clenched fists here I am now in my dwelling right under your nose.

Dwelling made from your impotence from the mere power of my moving from the freedom of my spermatozoids dwelling dark womb lined in red drapes the only altar I ever bless from where I can watch the world explode as pleases my silence

To the Serpent

At times in the bewilderment of cities I found myself wondering which animal to adore. Then I would go back to the primal eras. Undoing the cycles unlacing the knots defeating plots removing covers killing my hostages I searched.
Ferret. Tapir. Uprooter.
Where where where the animal that warned me of floods
Where where where the bird that led me to honey
Where where where the bird that showed me fountainheads
the memory of great alliances betrayed great friendships lost by our fault exalted me
Where where where
Where where where
Speech became cheap
O serpent sumptuous spine do you enclose my grandfather's powerful soul in your sinuous straps?
I salute you serpent through whom the morning shakes the beautiful mauve mane of December mangoes and for whom the milk-invented night tosses its luminous mice off its wall
I salute you serpent grooved like the seabed and which my heart I swear detaches to us as a premise of the flood
I salute you serpent your reptation is more majestic than *their* stride and the peace begrudged by their god you hold supremely.

Serpent frenzy and peace

over the hurdles of a malfeasant wind the land dismembers for me the secrets that made their steps resound at the outlet of the immemorially treacherous gorges they strangled

all rubbish! let them all rot until becoming the pennon of a black crow weakening in a waving of white wings.
Serpent
ample and regal disgust defeating the return to the sands of trickery
spindrift feeding the seagull's futile flit
to the pale tempest of soothing silences you the least frail warm yourself.
When the fire consuming the cape with the echoing burst flares up from the mourning bark

You bathe within the most discordant screams on the grass's spumous dreams
just to make the threat of your successive deaths—a green familiarity with the elements—
more fearsome.

Your threat yes your threat body rising from the raucous blur of bitterness where it fooled the worried lighthouse keeper whistling while he takes the time of a small gallop toward the murderous beams of discovery.

Serpent
seductive stinger of women's breasts and through whom death insinuates itself
maturity in the depth of a fruit sole lord only lord whose multiple image places on the cursed fig tree's altar an offering of tresses which is an octopodous threat which is a sagacious hand unforgiving to the cowards

The "fig tree's altar" is perhaps a reference to Matthew 21:19, in which Jesus, exhorting his disciples to faith, cursed a fruitless fig tree which then withered away.

Torture

All those whose heart is an ink spot on a child's notebook all those whose speech is an embrace broken in a last attempt at earthly gigantism
carry either on their hands a moon grooved by the scraping of glacial moraines or in their gait an evil snake crossing a zebra grid of circles and ellipses under the pretext of initiation
All those who know how to draw large stains of dark sperm along with the diagram of their fall over the imperial crimson cloak
all those whose fingers are a yet unseen magnificence of butterflies curved along the earth's axis
O all those whose eyes are a carousel of birds born from a superhuman balance between sponges and fragments of a galaxy extinguished under the heel of a small station

Pennon

In Seville the last bull's forehead pierced by an eyepiece
the sun oozing darkness at the pole
in the fjord the strangling of a rasp
in my throat a glass of cool water refusing to go down
My Lord executioner
for the Lord's sake
give me a hyena's small bite
in the name of mankind give me a small kick
in the name of the son as of the father poison my auricle
for your image you black bandit Almamy Samory it is on horseback that
I imagine it—
an old man and beating the final hiccup of a young and rough willfulness
against the flank of the native forest
and the dislocation of the last continent

Almamy Samory Touré, born in Guinea in 1830, fought against the French colonization of West Africa, especially in Sudan. Starting with an army of local rebels, he rose to become the king of the vast empire of Wassoulou, adding "Almamy," that is, "Commander of the Believers," to his name. Captured in 1898, he was exiled to Gabon, where he died in 1900.

Refinement of a Mummy

I embalmed my severed head in a very thin membrane
whose power of absorption remains to be calculated
maggots? thread? swaddles? at the other end ice packs or angels
Look I am so smooth you'd think no one ever looked at me
for sure I escaped the dogs, is it for nothing
there are sirens sounding clanging the roll call of cities
men who do not wait for the sappers of nothingness
and defrocked priests laughing up their sleeves
Astrologers
all your calculations are already in my miscalculations
                                        in pyramidal cubits
                                        in crying breathing capacity
and the cavern outlined by my lumbering steps always faces any polestar
No good-byes (from my hispid tongue)
a large bird sitting at my bedside deigned to turn away from me the formula
and the horrible feast
my neatly secured gesture
times the parallactic steps
like a block of ice in urine the earth breaks up
and with the innocent drift of its echo nurtures a beryl

Idyll

When the world reaches its evening and streetlamps become tall
immobile girls a yellow bow in their hair and a finger on their lips
when the light in the window cuts its braid and fries its eggs in a blood
drop congealed in the wounded's snow
when the heavy noon wine casts grain to the midnight stars there shall be
in my soul the fog's light corbels summoned to shed buckets of light
loneliness shall open tiny windows
over the fine radiophonic friendship of numbers
and in the calendar's reconversion in the bonfire of the days' printing
block

the daybreak shall be so bright the days will shine through

raven sweet servant
raucous and voluptuous just like me
booty of thick air and garrulous space there shall be
an auto's pump decapitated on the executioner's block time to play wolf
children's laughs from an unseen playground reminiscent of riding hoods
reminiscent
of the devoured ones
reminiscent
of the prophets men used to pelt out of their dreams with gray stones

raven
your day's coming purposelessly on makeshift limbs
like a black servant nimble milk carrier

raven
the last hanged man turns his legal eye in the chaste zero
of contrition and absurdity

raven sweet mandrake's song
venomous and tranquil like me
there still are the castle's blue stones to loosen
and the facile geometry of falsehood

raven
with your black signature honor the blank page
escaped from the slack season of virginal embraces

bullheaded raven

standing behind the trap of your croaking
when the scrupulous inventory of ordinary words begins
for it will be time to think of witnesses smoother than stars
—on what hooves did your form escape? my guardian angel shall say
arisen from the patience of the sidewalk and the brook's fire
near a leafy pond his earthly fingers sowing
in vain words tasting
of bread and booby traps

I shall not answer anything
but along the meridian shall lead him
to the chaste epiphany of a blood rosace of a forge's sheaf of light
where the great dusky push torques the black thrust amidst the
the white sand

then from the one that reminds their boa constrictor's vocation to the roads
strangling the scenery they were meant to nurse
to the one that makes my incorruptible life's sacred peacocks
murmur with reminiscence
the red oxen shall bring the day back to the tomb where a frothy
champagne flush glittering with buds and atolls
shall open languid palms
in the air there shall be as bearers of fair weather ocelli and crystal stags
great virgin words pious alligators
whose teeth shall be cleaned by our very wise birds

you sleep twister of roots
I irrigate your fields
collect the voice ordering the termites to build
high in my skull their funeral pyramid rigged with a flight
of iridescent pigeons

then you bird struck by the sling of mirages
knocking your head against the dome of the sun
of stars and dreams and nothingness
o you prisoner of your seal the pride of parchments
from island to island clear water you disdain
you shall fall
star bruiser grass cruncher great body

Password

Zeland I tune to your pitch
Zeland which never gives me quite enough time to arrange in the closet of my throat
all the words I had used to trap the days in an eviscerated calendar
Zeland in the depth of the shipwreck
Zeland surrounded by a strewing of carapaces
Zeland with your rosette of zinnias
Zeland the vibrating cilium of innocence
Zeland whose eyes are a watch stopped at some unreadable hour
Zeland a storm ill-corseted with black over the earth's fire
Zeland password
Zeland hippobroma
Zeland where antipodes meet
Zeland do not interrogate me
Zeland I no longer know my name
in the morning that rolls about the first impact of the first wreckage of the last dawn
our teeth will make an earth leap to the top of a sky of cinnamon and cloves
you will open your eyelids that are a splendid fan of feathers
reddened from watching my blood throb
a season triumphant with exceptional essences
that will be your hair
dangling the nostalgia of long cassia in the newborn wind

The Shape of Things

Seriously the fussings of birds of paradise no longer fade the wind rose
and when I open the cage of my eyelids when I release my hawks from
their gloved nest and triggering off my pupils hurl them where most
miraculously hunger's pollen discretely achieves the fecundation of
despair's sterile flower
(froth from speech thoughtlessly thrown amidst the fire of a silence
barely perceived mass of my left breast overly robust outgrowth of my
toes' wildest exercise
dragging the worlds' odds and ends to my liking
to my liking quicksanding weaker and weaker gasps which I arrange
nicely into docile defunct worlds)
justice to the scenery! It's he the screamer he again
the path smiles to itself in the sunsets
the stones tame the raging sea
the crabs those sewers' suns rebelling against the street sweepers' system
are hanging from the top of ancient palaces
my clenched hands pass the axe of forebodings to each other
The city? A city's emptiness. The city? Emptiness of eyes emptiness of
nightmares emptiness of memory emptiness of indifference

Preliminary Question

As for me let them squeeze my leg
and I'll disgorge a forest of lianas
Let them hang me by the nails
and I'll piss a camel carrying a pope and
I'll fade into a row
of ficuses that crush the intruder very nicely and strangle him in a beautiful tropical swaying
The weakness of many men is they do not know how to become either a stone or a tree
As for me I sometimes insert sulfur fuses between my boa fingers for the sole pleasure of bursting all evening long into the blaze of new poinsettias leaves
red and green fluttering in the wind
as in my throat our dawn

Tattooing Eyes

Eyes hooked to their high hypertrophied peduncle cashew tree's eyes and
tannin pus leveled at me like a rotten fruit's eyes like slaughterhouse flies
like an executioner's beard
indeed I am the most pierced being in the world
each man on my path grabbing the right to drive a nail just anywhere
into my head my heart my hands my eyes

but my great joy is to parry their strikes: ferociousness of my inner self
right where
they expected finding a void—void sand and termite-crumbled wood
instead of the alburnum I fashion for myself regardless of the season—

Poorly anchored they sink
whereas my ink arching its back and cooing resurfaces as sap to give me a
color under which to wait in comfort (in this forest where one has to be a
blockhead like Christ and cabbage to be crucified) and ambush the inane
larcenous tricks of the forever lurking nails

Forfeit

As soon as I press the little catch I have under my tongue beneath
its triple layer of false eyelashes of centuries of insults of madrepore
strata of what I must call my niagara cavern in a place free from any
detection any microscopic bombardment or soothsayer's divination or
scientific prospection in an explosion of cockroaches a cobra's spasm
as in astonishment a tongue leaps up like a machine meant to spit a
mouthful of curses a backup of hellish sewers a premonitory ejaculation
a urinary spurt a foul emission a sulfuric rhythm feeding uninterrupted
interjections—and then see pushing between the cobblestones are
the petrol's tumultuous blue eucalypti that leave the splendor of the
veronicas far behind them, the skulls smack on the delirious dust like the
jaboticaba plum and then in a loud buzzing of hornets begins the real
war of devolution in which all is fair game there soar the fire's homing
pigeons there comes the crackling of secret radios and the thick billows
of black smoke resembling vaginal adenoids propelled into the air by the
pelvic thrust of coit. I count. Across the street a honey-colored armillate
lay down dwarflike on its side an uprooted church reduced by disaster to
its true urinal proportions. I cross over collapsed bridges. I walk under
new arches. An eye sleds down a cheek amidst well-maintained wood and
brass work a house right on the abyss in its section the house daughter's
raped maidenhood the lost goods and chattels of the father and mother
who believed in human dignity and at the bottom of a wool stocking
the testicles of an unemployed worker from distant lands pierced with a
knitting needle.
My hand goes to my forehead it is a spawning of monsoons. My hand
goes to my dick. It has vanished into fumes of foliage. Deserting the sky
the whole light has taken refuge in the red-hot white-hot yellow-hot
stripes of serpents mindful of the decaying of this landscape spurned by
dogs' piss.
What's the use?
The planets are very fast breeding birds which at any moment
majestically release their guano silos on its spit
the earth vomits alternately the grease of each of its halves

handfuls of fish hang up their emergency lights to the pilasters of stars whose ancient sliding crumbles away into the dark as a dense and very bitter coca odor.

Who among you has never happened to strike a land because of its inhabitants' malice? Today I stand up and in the only whiteness men have ever granted me.

To the Night

It must be that woman whose place and date of apparition were revealed to me by astrology and geomancy
and whom I had overlooked
and whose voice backlights the ponds awkwardly caught in the nets of bulrushes
backlights the suicide's blast furnaces
backlights the barnacles hanging up a large bunch of jonquils from the rocks as a sign spring is here
when the wind has blown a piece of tissue paper
onto an old comb when on it the wind
that oldest of old niggers blows a tune in which
nice fables stick their legs out of a heather made of the lovable wool of wolves
pirating dog's ramblings

or else that one crowned Iroise Straight standing and awaiting from me words
signifying *nothing to fear* which for sure will not happen
it is Grace or Disgrace
it is the heart's little trot in the horological illness named Basedow's
it is Grace it's Disgrace
Disgrace or Rancor
Rancor with its deaf man's teeth laying out its net of jagged teeth like undergrowth unfolding at the auricles' mystery

Rancor pounding out its words sweeping all bets away
Rancor made in the likeness of God who creates with small stabs
simmering in wait of orders from a sheath frozen in guiac gum
or no more
than

you raise your face
the first communion's thin trickle of blood

I do not spill

no more

than my petrous face rises when hiding its most harmless liaisons

no more than one would necessarily expect rancor from our badly
stitched faces that leach the sight more probable
than the smile in which from veins and arteries we mingle our two
bloods
and their words of unequal strength

Antipodal Dwelling

Crucible where the world is born meshes of the fresh earth
first hair founding stone of our worry
when the rain becomes the thread which the world unravels ply by ply
when the sun becomes a spider in which to lose ourselves one by one
when the sea becomes an octopus spitting out our hopes in our faces
when the moon uncoils and unwinds for us its long serpent's body
when the volcano shakes the wrinkles off its pachydermic body
when the wind stops blowing as someone forgot to strike the wind stones
when having preached too long in the desert the stones stop talking
(raveling my veins the whole forest from its lowest branches raveling my veins
all of the water and the pattern of faithful fires
raveling from its depth will throw water lilies into my face and my redemption blood and my shoulders more slippery than any slipknot raveling
water drop in the precious still of aquifers which will open their windows and shout the weather is fine in the ill-understood Esperanto of the striated curls of our most bitter sputum) drop of fire in the wind's hazardless throat
firefly and water I will build myself out of tiny drops of fire water too beautiful for another architect

dwelling made of water glanced at on awaking
dwelling made of puckered perfumes
dwelling made of spangled slumbers
dwelling made of torpid lizards' swollen throats
force aligns me on the shadeless meridian

pythons teams of disaster unnatural brothers of my longitude
the roads rise to the occasion
on the platform of the compass's runaway sky
green-eyed gnomides losing track of their prayers take aim at us

dwelling made of the laying of palms
dwelling made of cheetahs' red eyes
dwelling made of a shower of sand shells

this time the gunshots give me an aura too large for my head whose loose parts are arriving by portage

Fresh Out of a Metamorphosis

Last gasp of the dying man in the last ray of the sun
Jamblique oblique
and
pope
In Shanghai let us collect the children's skeletons offered by the shovel to famine's ferocious beasts
but the wintering but your birdlimed hair sticking to your eyes and the tufted stenches arising from your thighs more virginal than the forests
would be useless in the razzias of the release of Indonesian plates
when India and the Ganges (tsunami tsunami) play hide-and-seek with Krakatoa
My friend tsunami and you Ganges granary of tubers for underwater harvests
my wild one
my grandiose one
fresh out of a metamorphosis let us emerge in a light rain on a Chicago street on the odd numbers side
with a brain reborn from the slaughterhouse and a hand free from mercury
and who cares if the visibility worsens
our fists are clenched on hygienic confidence
at dawn in the evening
the fusion is more intense and more intimate than at any moment of dusk
at this hour precisely incredibly potent
when in bed and at the latitude of the Tropic of Cancer
the formidable copulation of the squid and the sperm whale ignites and continues in the wine of drunken gashes and gushes

crippled the men we encounter
as you know hunchbacks are the best antidote against priests

Jamblique of Chalcis was a third-century Neoplatonic philosopher. Judged heretical by the fathers of the Christian church, his doctrine influenced the Gnostics through a synthesis of intellect and senses.

Like a Misunderstood Salvation

Obsidian Stele for Alioune Diop

For your sake, my brother, I assembled you as a bird
an African grouse able to cross unharmed the hottest desert sands
an African coliou able to foil the wiles of scrubland and confront
the laughter
of the forest
trekker of dunes
your crest erected in a surge of pride
you knew how to fly high
a major migrant
you knew how to fly far
above all high
in one sole glance embracing
the hereditary patrimony to its most remote parcel
inspector of lost inheritances
testate of loyalties
a daily dealer opened only to undiscovered hopes and vast memories
whose benefits festered in the depth or wintered beyond the subtlety of
each one of your gestures

obsidian of memory
man of the rescript
man of the rod

the Message
through the dust of confines
and the crest and the swell
you held it at all times above your head
your arm held out of the mire
your heart out of beats
out of the fear
faithful to the inner command.

(April 20, 1983)

Alioune Diop (1910–1980) was cofounder of the journal *Présence Africaine* and publishing house by the same name in 1947 and 1949, respectively.

Passage

What I tally here is the compulsory passage
the end of the listing
a rumination of low tides
the inventory as well of lengthy droughts
on the flaccid teats of the peaks.

the very configuration of the miracle certifies sufficiently
the obvious face of vomit

cirques and coves
final synthesis of gorges and sea shelves
I know it rests with me
to pacify a spring misled into vast wanderings
to salvage
what remains
to salvage the living
                    magma of the word even stronger from its silences

References

Espouser of the place
rather than looking for
an alibi
he scanned the scenery into which to encrust himself

let erosion erode him
let the trade winds slap him
(him totally morne, totally volcano)

the consistency of the journey was not affected
shortcuts being no more than scars of landslides
gropingly he was drawing
the fragile chance that faced the sun

a mummy of mud

Supreme Mask

To dress the mask of words
with fibers feather silky woods

with stone copper iron
to surge
around my neck the collar of memory

up to the debilitated dawn
up to the loftiest conjuncture
where in a primal zone
the wild mutation of mobile continents
combine

bearer of the most powerful mask

The Virtue of Fireflies

Not losing hope in fireflies
I acknowledge that as virtue.
pursuing hunting for them
keep watching for them.
the dream is not to fix them into torches
nor that they might match noncold lights
in any case I bet that reconversion takes place
somewhere for all those
who have never accepted the air's sluggishness

I am glad the transmission of hiccups of truth
happens gropingly
and paroxysmically
otherwise it would inevitably sink into
the inept babbling of the ambient marshland

Rumination

Must know how to decipher their shadow
even if their churchbell not unrelated to the diving bell
becomes your sole way to tell the time

must valorize their bad manners
their becoming crazed gods in drunkenness

their beauty is of the savage kind
unexpected always.
must listen. Probe the labyrinth.

I listen along the imperious blood that ascends
through the wreckage the faluns the jetsam
to the faithful sap.

            I do not argue
I welcome the words (safeguarding the sound's serum)
I know their memory, what they owe me:
everything need I say more

I sometimes create islands
from calderas overflowing with orange groves

Time to Speak

How many rivers
mountains
seas
                    disasters
To think how many centuries
                    the forests

time to speak:
                    quicksands spiral on and on
                    only what's hard is tillable

dance memory dance
the unlivable into its suitable site

move on lead on
let the caravan of mornes fall asleep on the horizon
the lion of the north belch its entrails
at the crossroad amidst the lava cooled off too soon
you shall encounter the child

it is the wind I mean

with an ample lungful follow him a long way
move on

                    on your path
ignore the dogs
the wind alive through you suffices to flesh them

with all of the mountain that was built up in you
construct each step flustering
the slumbering rubble

do not defile the pure face of the future
builder of a different tomorrow

let not your thread get entangled
let not your voice tire out
let not your paths narrow down

move on

Course

with my strict saliva I kept the blood flowing
so it would not waste in oblivious squamae
on uncertain seas I rode
the dolphins of memory
heedless of everything
except for recording the reef
duly logging the landmark
for the wrecking of gods I reinvented words
wherever I landed I ploughed the fallow
dug the furrow fashioned the talus
here and there poking o hope
white tip after white tip
the humble dubbing of your bitter burgeon

Dyali

for Léopold Sédar Senghor

if the liana bridge collapses
it'll be on a swarm of sea-urchin stars
you'd believe one less could not have
goaded our draft oxen's steps
nor lit our nights
that I remember
and in the already faint echoing
that snarling in us of most ancient felines

Then loneliness may well arise
out of the throng of old curses
and step onto the shores of remembrance
amidst the uncovered shoals
and the raveled ravings of islands
still I shall not forget the words
of the dyali

dyali
through the dune and the wear and tear
conveyer of sap and verdant tenderness
inventor of the people and their burgeon
their sentinel for the trade winds
master of their words
you are saying *dyali*
and *Dyali* I say as well
sayer of the essential
always to be told again
and then as in the olden days
here comes untiring honor

Here is confronting Time
a new passage to discover
a new breach to open
in opacity in darkness in hardness
and here's a new sheaf of constellations to locate

new halts new fountainheads
for the hunger for the thirst of forgotten birds

and here
Here comes
Dyali

the peasant's patience in pushing the seeds
and the stubbornness of conspiring roots

deep into the earth
deep into the heart
the sun erazed
for blazon

The term "dyali" is Césaire's distortion of the Senegalese "djali" or "djeli," referring to a griot, that is, a praise singer-cum-minstrel. Léopold Sédar Senghor (1906–2001) was a very early friend of Césaire's in Paris and cofounder of the journal *L'étudiant noir.* He published *Anthology of New Negro and Malagasy Poetry* in 1948 and became the first president of independent Senegal in 1960. The word "erazed" (also erased and arranché) is a heraldic term referring to the part of an animal (lion, eagle, or ram) represented by a jagged lower edge as if torn from the rest of the body.

Rapacious Space

Thyrses-trunks
Drapings
Conventicles of sylvan gods
The extraterrestrial chatter of the tree ferns

Here and there the blood-red exhibitionism
Of impassive balisiers
A rapacious display
(ferocious or sumptuous
the quest is a thirst for being)

Soon will come the game of pale gold castaneas
Then the simaruba trunks burnt alive

Let them gesticulate some more
Theater in the dust of female fire
They are the hills' last fawn wrestlers

Minister-of-the-pen of this very strange court
To say that I walk this domain day and night
Is not enough
When it is he that summons and needs me
As guardian

To make sure that all is there
Intact absurd
The fairy's lantern
Cocoons needfully loamy
That it all at once flares up with unfathomed meaning
Whose dictate I never could inflect in me.

Phantasms

Starting up is not done at a blustering space
It remains entangled in the early morning
And its ordinary accoutrement of fog
The collusion of silence took care of the whole lot
I mean a throng of screams under the iron heel

Serpent screams
Rattler screams
Lizard screams awaiting the sun
Desiccated phasms screams

Beside the everyday screams there are the forever
Screams
Those stand up haughtily
Posted in the vague concern for their testimony
Girdled in the armor of their role

Screams locusts of devouring solitudes.

Laughable

letter to a faraway friend

I have not been nailed to the most absurd of rocks
No winged exploit ever visited me
Out of the abyss no chorus rises toward me
Except at times the hiccup of a shipwrecked boatload
No use mentioning
That I don't give a damn about a civil status
established obviously from mere nostalgia
I have not been scarred by some obliging beak
Threatened with some serious retaliation
otherwise
The difficulties with hindsight
being easily compensated by the broadening of sight
I do not graze on panic
I do not ruminate on remorse
All I do is peck at the ordinary season
Waiting the time of a brief flash
(that time called idle)
the wake of a lost acquiescence
or shall we say an injunction
PS:
But given all vigor has vanished
That the tide is reluctant
The trade winds dying on me
That even pollen and sand fail to reach me
untouched
If between myself and myself
the futile track startles and turns in circles
In one fell swoop let my silence alone
Deliver me into the lap of the land
The ill-deciphered jubilation
of a solitary magma
Horseman of time and sea foam

Craters

The possibility of a swift ending vanishes for lack of lava, along rivers too pebbly to escape notice from thirsty snakes.

Blood-gorged Fury hurled until when the merciless track fades out in the quasi-autumnal fog.

It does not fool me.

Misery will not tire playing leapfrog over the craters, even if it relents during a brief flash in some suicidal volcano's effusion.

Conventicles

Enough nibbling of sunrise
enough furling of sunset
And the animals will have fled
carrying out of the city
its last secret to warmth.
At this point we're only just
talking
of discovering a door
by groping through
the devastation of the local compost
towards the speed of perilous tenderness
which makes the tree my resolute brother
The wind my surf-shredding brother
The volcano my nauseous brother
And the ceaselessly stifled sobbing
of the surf

Islands Speak

a salute to Édouard Maunick

If we wish for the bee to breed again in the blood's campeachy wood

If we wish to disentangle the ponds and the water hyacinths

If we wish to drive back the tree-climbing crabs devourers of leaves

If we wish to turn the rust and dust of dreams into an avalanche of dawn

What are you . . .

You who understand what islands say

And that they converse in the margins of seas and behind the lands' back
in their secret jargon of algae and birds

What are you assisting the fire the flood and the blowing

What did you come to tell us so violently and tenderly

If not that within reach of the voice

Within reach of the hand and the conch

Within reach of the heart and heroism

Speaking farther speaking higher raises the sword tree and the sword
Hope on the rim of an abyss

Living harvests of Memory.

Édouard Maunick (b. 1931) is a Mauritian poet, contributor to the journal *Présence Africaine,* and recipient of the Grand Prix de la Francophonie from the French Academy in 2003. The zoological meaning of the French word "appareiller" is to match animals for breeding purposes. In this poem, Césaire coins the word "réappareiller" as way of expressing the idea of "breeding again."

Like a Misunderstood Salvation

from grievance to grievance
from remembrance to remanence
from stitch to stitch
at full tilt
from sea to sea
from evil master to evil master
from the sanguineous song of coral trees
to the age-old thirst of the stubborn stream of incense
as for you solstice
right in the middle of the mêlée
encampment of a herd of vendible volcanoes
crush me with obstinate odors
scattered
from roads moist with amaryllis
to a bush of scorched rubble
                makes no difference
the labyrinth regresses from the cloudy future
to the night of stingily opened fountains
                blemish
                        blunder
fades away like a misunderstood salvation

In the original French version, Césaire uses the word "marâtre," which in English means "stepmother," probably a reference to the evil motherland associated with metropolitan France. However, the context of slavery is also implicit in the poem, and we have therefore chosen to use "evil master" as a way of emphasizing this connection.

Ruminatings of Calderas

Array
of being and thirst
or rather disarray

an alphabet at bay

at the hour when in the wind
there are the storm's sharks
flashing their silver throats
the time it takes for one leap
the unbelievable uprootings of cecropias
at the hour when in the wind and amidst the foliage
there are great whirlings of shamans and joltings
at the hour when in the wind
there's always the great exorcist
the most powerful of ceibas
the fetish athlete of a town to be destroyed
bracing up the sliding hill
always in the nick of time
embracing it
and bracing the roots
at the hour when in the wind
there are shiverings
but also the imperturbable anguish woven red
in the heart of balisiers
still it is not too late
to climb back the ample swell of defiance and angers
by way of relieving the patience of colors
in the reptation of lianas
and the always mirthful mood
of deep-sea geneses.

Through

Exalting their serene splendor into arborescence
a row of young women
opened the path for me gracefully tipping down
their green umbrellas
ferns, ferns
hurly-burly also of lands sores and swellings
I saw a rainbow hide rather than surrender
in the basalt jaws of an unperturbed
cave
I saw the disaster serpent and bull crawling
leaping and stopping dead restrained by a frail
arbuscule in its earing season
I saw the quest of a forgotten dream disturb time
unravel the labyrinth
I saw a flight of rapacious buzzards
snouts and beaks in support
dispute my nights
shred by shred
ground down to sand
then the time came for the mountain
to settle on the horizon
a beheaded lion harnessed with all our wounds.

The Sleeping Woman Rock, or *Beautiful Like the Exasperation of the Secession*

Survivor survivor
It is you the fallout
From some feasting of volcanoes
From a whirling of fireflies
From a flare of flowers a furor of dreams

So pure away from all that jungle
The tow of your hair lit up
To the very bottom of the solar barque
Exasperation of the secession

From time to time through the clearing
Sand mist
Through the sky's scarified games
I see her batting her eyes
Just to let me know she understands my signals
Which are moreover in distress about the fallings of a very
Ancient sun

As for hers I am alone I believe in still intercepting them
More than once I encouraged the wave
To cross the space persistent between us
But the dragon steers the course of this forbidden water
Even if it is often as a harmless hawksbill
That it comes up for air on the fateful surface

So what sacrificial bird should I send you
Today

Survivor survivor
You my exile and queen of this rubble
Ghost forever inapt at completing her kingdom

According to Annick Thébia-Melsan, the rounded hills of volcanic origin in the south of the island of Martinique reminded Aimé Césaire of the shape of a woman asleep. See "Pour que continue l'aventure commune," in *Aimé Césaire: Pour regarder le siècle en face,* ed. Annick Thébia-Melsan (Paris: Maisonneuve & Larose, 2000), 6.

Favor from the Trade Winds

(*prose for the Sun*)

It is inadequate.

Sometimes losing its mind it is reduced to a morbid crab, contentedly self-absorbed in the mute neighing of its beams. In this case it is the wind that stirs it up, the wind, and keeps it from settling in the heaviness of peoples.
Of flowers I will say that they focus on what no one would assume to be their perfume.
That's the trap.
The sun, weighs, shows off.

The wind disperses it, disconcerts it, freedom.

For a Fiftieth Anniversary

for Lilyan Kesteloot

Exceed exude exult Elan
Presence we must build your evidence
on buttresses of pachira
on an obelisk
on a crater for a sparrow hawk
on a sunbeam
on copaiba essence
almost anything
on a caravelle stern
on a fleet of almadias
on favellas
on citadels
on andesite ramparts
on an entanglement of peaks
anything
the wind inexpert at remembering meanders
is stung
to the quick that my breath
my breath alone suffices
to signify to all
now and forever
that a man was here
and that a torch in the heart of nights
a banner in the heart of the day
a standard
a simple hand offered
he cried out
an unforgettable wound.

Lilyan Kesteloot, former director of research at the Institut Fondamental d'Afrique Noire in Dakar, Senegal, was a lifelong friend and critic of Césaire's. Her publications include *Les écrivains noirs de langue française: Naissance d'une littérature* (*Black Writers in French: A Literary History of Negritude,* 1963) and *Anthologie négro-africaine* (1967). This poem celebrates the fiftieth anniversary of the French publication of the *Cahier d'un retour au pays natal* (*Notebook of a Return to a Native Land*).

Configurations

for Jacqueline Leiner

1

murmur
    of musty mangle smells
    of splintered husks
                        of airborne seeds

murmur of anchor-deep seeds so clever
at plotting the torture of a land

(and too bad for those who do not understand
the forever slippery gravity of this game
of driftings and groundings)

beacons we are told condescendingly provided

    gallop of all startled beasts
    rushed from the beginning of time

        the tongue of fire
        the word
        the exasperated benevolent asp of tender human milk

2

When I wake up feeling grand as a mountain
no need to look around. It's clear.
More Pelée-like than age would justify.

At other times finding myself like a tatou
I of course sneak into Caravel
all lights and beacons extinguished
hugging the deceptive doldrums of freebooting

Jacqueline Leiner (1921–2008) was a professor of Romance languages and comparative literature at the University of Tübingen and a longtime friend and supporter of Césaire's.

Now and then it is a blossoming cane field that contrives
me a plume on my head.
Libra that is not the good sign.
For I expect a stunting mildew to hit me
any moment.

My better days are when
an unscrupulous, infuriated and cynical whirlwind,
sneering for every prey hemmed in the claws
of my turmoil,

I leap

    blind
    bound for death
    berserk.

Those are my glorious days
                enraged
                        vengeful

3
Nothing ever delivers save the opacity of words

Words of decency and indecency
Words of severe sayings.

Coiling of the great thirst of being
spiral of the great urge and great downturn of being
knot of seaweeds and entrails
knot of the rising and ebbing of being.
I forgot: words as well for slack waters:
which are in a knot the rage of not saying.

Torpor does not speak.
Thick. Heavy. Gross.
A precipitate. Who dared?
the quicksanding has reached its limit.

At the limit of the muck.
ah!
there is no uttering but from a jump start.
To smash the muck.
To smash.
Rendition of a delirium binding the whole universe
to the uprising of a rock!

4
This space scrawled on by the restless lava
I surrender to Time.
(Time which is nothing else than sluggishness of speech)

the fissure
any rupture
even the momentary wound inflicted
by the guiltless bug

The very crack which life did not fill
all shall be found there in the end
gathered for the obliging sand

Please at the entrance of the cave acknowledge
a slab of red jasper
murdered in full daylight
blood clot

Avant-Garde & Modernism Studies

Avant-Garde & Modernism Collection